# MUNICIPAL FINANCIAL REPORTING
# AND DISCLOSURE QUALITY

RONALD M. COPELAND
Northeastern University

ROBERT W. INGRAM
University of Iowa

# MUNICIPAL FINANCIAL REPORTING AND DISCLOSURE QUALITY

ADDISON-WESLEY PUBLISHING COMPANY
Reading, Massachusetts • Menlo Park, California
London • Amsterdam • Don Mills, Ontario • Sydney

This book is in the
Addison-Wesley Paperback Series in Accounting
Consulting Editor
William J. Bruns, Jr.

**Library of Congress Cataloging in Publication Data**

Copeland, Ronald M.
   Municipal financial reporting and disclosure quality.

   (The Addison-Wesley paperback series in accounting)
   Includes bibliographies and indexes.
   1. Municipal finance—Accounting.   2. Disclosure in
accounting.   I. Ingram, Robert W.   II. Series.
III. Title.
HJ9773.C66   1983        657'.835        82-11580
ISBN 0-201-10197-1

ISBN 0-201-10197-1
ABCDEFGHIJ-DO-89876543

# EDITOR'S FOREWORD

The environment for accounting has undergone revolutionary changes in the last decade. Demand for accountability by managers of both public and private organizations has risen significantly. Electronic data transmission, storage, and processing and other information technologies have developed to allow accountants to use methods and processes that would have been considered impossible, or uneconomical, just a few years ago. At the same time, new quantitative methods for solving accounting problems have been developed, and the behavioral sciences have suggested that the impact of accounting goes well beyond the systems and reports, which are the most visible product of the accountant's work.

The speed with which these developments have occurred has made it difficult for teachers and students of accounting, and for managers and accountants themselves, to keep their knowledge up-to-date. New solutions to problems, and sometimes even new kinds of accounting problems themselves, are not treated in many textbooks. In addition, problems and solutions often cross boundaries between what were once considered separate disciplines of study. The student or manager seeking a learning aid in an era of change will frequently be frustrated. In many respects, materials which have been available do not reflect either the new developments or the unprecedented opportunities for creative thinking and problem solving which accounting presents.

Each book in this Addison-Wesley Series treats a new development or subject that has not been widely treated in textbooks that are widely available. In addition, because each book concentrates on a single set of problems, methods, or topics in accounting, each provides comprehensive coverage in an economical form. The Series was conceived to help all who work with or process accounting information, all of whom must continue to learn in order to keep pace with the changes which are occurring. Each book has been carefully developed by an outstanding scholar.

Books in this Series were prepared in the belief that the evaluation of accounting and its importance to managers will continue, and with faith that books are an effective means to assist all who are interested to participate in the developments which will take place in the future. Our goal has been to improve the practice and processes of accounting, and to help all who use accounting information to do so more effectively.

William J. Bruns, Jr.
Professor of Business
Administration
Harvard University

# PREFACE

We have attempted in this book to synthesize research bearing on the quality of municipal disclosure. Our synthesis extends beyond the mere review of existing accounting literature; in fact, two-thirds of the references in our bibliography are found in the literature of other disciplines. Many persons besides accountants have a vital interest in the municipal financial reporting environment, including governmental administrators, municipal creditors, taxpayers, and other constituents. This book is addressed to those who wish to know more about research findings on municipal accounting disclosure quality, but who may have neither the time nor the inclination to read the original papers on the subject. Municipal disclosure quality is of increasing concern to academics and professionals interested in government and accounting.

Our book is not meant to be a definitive treatment of municipal disclosure quality. On the contrary, the monograph is intended to provide interested readers with an initial exposure to a broad body of literature on a complex subject. We hope the approach is distinctive, so that readers may gain insight into the nature of municipal financial reporting. Our attempt is designed to illuminate obscure issues concerned with several dimensions of municipal disclosure quality. Although we presume that the reader is familiar with municipal operations and accounting, our discussion is broad enough to accommodate unsophisticated readers.

Each chapter is based, in part, on some of our previous writings. The primary sources from which materials are drawn, both those written by us and others, are contained in detailed bibliographies, which can provide guidance to those interested in pursuing selected topics in greater depth. Five bibliographies are contained in this book: the first four concentrate on specialized topics, and the last one contains information on the remaining references cited in the text. An Author Index is provided to help readers trace references.

Research on municipal accounting is growing at an unprecedented rate and is being published in a variety of sources. Much research has been conducted, and not all of it is reviewed here. Moreover, new research results are published with each issue of leading academic journals, but we effectively terminated our evaluation of the literature as of February 1982. Hence new research findings that both support and contradict those reported in this volume will be found in the literature published after our cutoff date.

We wish to express our appreciation to the many individuals whose contributions are reflected in this volume. First, we acknowledge the efforts of our coauthors of various papers dealing with municipal accounting issues, especially Roy Brooks and Rick Ellson of the University of South Carolina and Julia Magann of the University of Texas. Next, we thank those who read substantial portions of this manuscript and gave us helpful comments, particularly Julia Magann of the University of Texas, Kris Raman of North Texas State University, Alan Drebin of Northwestern University, Robert Parry of Indiana University, and John Engstrom of Northern Illinois University. Nick Dopuch, Steve Zeff, and Allen Schick have all provided valuable editorial suggestions that improved the quality of articles reporting our original research efforts. Comments of the unnamed referees for the *Journal of Accounting Research, The Accounting Review,* and *Public Budgeting and Finance* are also acknowledged. Some of our original work was presented at several workshops, and we express our appreciation for the feedback received from the participants at Indiana University, Purdue University, Sloan School at MIT, Northeastern University, Boston University, the University of Texas, the University of Georgia, and the University of Iowa.

We also wish to acknowledge the support of Dave Blake and Jim Kane, both of whom provided an administrative climate conducive to writing this book. An extra measure of thanks is due to Frank Burns, sponsoring editor at Addison-Wesley, and Bill Bruns, editor of this series, both of whom provided advice and encouragement.

*Boston, Massachusetts*                                              R. M. C.
*Iowa City, Iowa*                                                        R. W. I.
*November 1982*

# CONTENTS

# MUNICIPAL FINANCIAL REPORTING
# AND DISCLOSURE QUALITY

*Chapter One*

# INTRODUCTION

The growing controversy concerning the adequacy of municipal financial disclosure may affect the well-being of all citizens in the United States. Accounting information is used, along with other data, in formulating decisions about the allocation of resources within our society and in evaluating the stewardship performance of elected officials. Some observers are entirely satisfied with the quality of municipal account disclosures currently available. Others claim that the quality of such disclosures is poor and that this condition fosters a misallocation of public resources, threatens the fiscal viability of cities, and undermines the effectiveness of elected officials. Many critics advocate change in contemporary municipal accounting and/or reporting practices, as well as in the institutions that promulgate municipal accounting standards. Introducing major change in practice, standards, or institutions is likely to affect decisions about allocation of resources, and these in turn may affect the welfare of many citizens (for better or for worse).

The positions advocated on both sides of the controversy frequently are not supported by systematic research evidence for the following reasons (the list is not exhaustive):

1. Many advocates have vested interests in the positions they take.
2. Assessing the quality of municipal disclosures is more difficult than assessing the quality of corporate disclosures, since more diversity exists in municipal disclosures.

3. Much of the research on municipal disclosure is published outside the accounting literature, and many accountants are unfamiliar with this research.

4. The focus of municipal research is often broader than its corporate counterpart, in part because the municipal constituency is less homogeneous than the corporate constituency.

5. Even when research evidence is fully accepted by all contesting advocates, policy implications of the findings still may be obscure.

Although each of these points will be discussed briefly in this chapter, the major focus of this book is to synthesize the diverse body of municipal disclosure research and to relate the evidence to questions concerning the quality of municipal financial accounting and reporting. Rather than being exhaustive, this review is intended to provide readers with a background from which they may initiate further study.

The institutional environment of municipal accounting and reporting is highly complex, perhaps even more complex than the environment for corporate financial disclosure. The municipal financial disclosure environment is characterized by an uncoordinated authority decentralized over several public and private sector arbiters of disclosure standards. Widespread disagreement exists on numerous issues, although consensus has been achieved on some elements of municipal reporting objectives. Advocates from each institution of authority have a vested interest in supporting positions that accrue more power to their institutional base. The institutional environment of municipal accounting will be discussed in the next section of this chapter. That discussion identifies the arbiters of municipal accounting standards and describes three points of consensus among all groups.

In contrast to corporate disclosures, municipal financial reporting practices are not regulated by a centralized federal authority such as the Securities and Exchange Commission. Diversity in disclosure is much more common for municipal annual reports than for corporate financial statements, as is described in more detail in Chapter 2. Lack of cross-sectional comparability is one consequence of diversity.

Many research studies containing financial accounting data as independent variables have been published in the political science, sociology, public finance, and finance literatures. Although some of these studies are directly relevant to current accounting concerns, they often have been ignored in the accounting literature. For example, Fabricant (1952) studied the determinants of municipal expenditures decades ago in research that is pertinent to municipal budgeting issues, but little reference to Fabricant (and the voluminous subsequent research) is to be found in the accounting literature. (See the classified bibliography in this book for references on determinants of municipal revenues and expenditures.) As another example, Downs (1957) formulated a positive theory describing what motivates elected officials to disclose information about municipal financial performance. Downs also discussed what motivates voters to obtain financial information about municipal operations. These issues and the subsequent empirical research were virtually ignored in the accounting literature until the early 1980s. (See Chapter 3 for an exposition of the research linking accounting data and voting outcomes.)

The municipal constituency is less homogeneous than the corporate counterpart. One element of the constituency, bondholders, is common to both municipal and corporate reporting. (Chapter 4 describes research linking accounting data with municipal bond ratings, changes in municipal bond ratings, and municipal bond yields.) Otherwise, the constituencies differ, primarily because corporate accounting systems capture information that is also reflected in competitive capital and product markets, while municipal accounting information is not reflected in analogous market data. That is, municipal accounting numbers are not validated by the market, since no market measures are available for public goods and services or for municipal equity interests (securities). However, municipal research has considered financial variables as explanatory elements in predicting and describing migration and fiscal stress, two phenomena that are weakly analogous to market phenomena. (See the classified bibliography for references on these two subjects.)

Municipal accounting data also satisfy the internal information needs of administrators charged with the responsibility of providing public goods and services to diverse constituencies. Accounting systems record, classify, and summarize transactions and other relevant events. Operating activities such as tax collection and payroll are captured by the accounting system and used by municipal administrators in planning and controlling activities for which they are responsible. Although much research has considered the use of accounting for promoting managerial efficiency and effectiveness, discussion of this literature is beyond the scope of this study. However, a classified bibliography on this subject is provided at the end of the book.

The policy implications of empirical accounting research are rarely clear-cut, even when a study is accepted as being without methodological fault. Policy often hinges upon variables that are exogenous to the research, for example, organizational goals. Policy implications stemming from the research described in this book are considered in Chapter 5.

The quality of municipal financial disclosures must be evaluated in light of the institutional environment in which disclosure standards are established. This environment is examined in the following section.

## SETTING STANDARDS FOR MUNICIPAL ACCOUNTING, REPORTING, AND AUDITING

Promulgations of three public sector and three private sector institutions may determine the accounting, reporting, and auditing standards that are applicable to a particular municipality. Public sector standards stem from federal, state, and local laws or guidelines. Private sector standards reflect promulations issued by the National Council on Governmental Accounting (NCGA), the Financial Accounting Standards Board (FASB), and the American Institute of Certified Public Accountants (AICPA). The relationship between municipal financial disclosures and these arbiters of disclosure practices is diagrammed in Exhibit 1.1 and described in more detail below.[1] Our description focuses on the basis that each institution has legitimate power to establish standards, since mandated practices can impact on disclosure quality.

### State and local legislation

Municipal governments are created under the incorporation statutes prescribed by the states in which they are located. Therefore,

**Exhibit 1.1**
**Regulation of municipal accounting procedures**

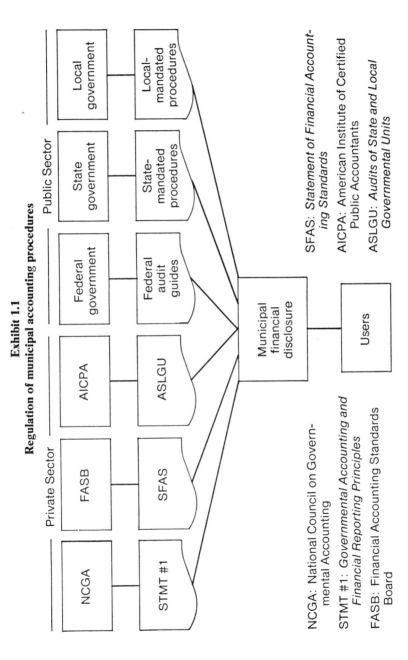

NCGA: National Council on Governmental Accounting

STMT #1: *Governmental Accounting and Financial Reporting Principles*

FASB: Financial Accounting Standards Board

SFAS: *Statement of Financial Accounting Standards*

AICPA: American Institute of Certified Public Accountants

ASLGU: *Audits of State and Local Governmental Units*

municipalities are subject to the accounting, reporting, and auditing constraints specified in state statutes. State regulation of municipal disclosure may be designed to standardize and strengthen accounting procedures; to insure that financial reports are complete, accurate, objective, and timely; and to insure that local officials responsible for public funds provide the public with an accounting of their stewardship.[2] Although legislation on disclosure in most states agrees with these broad objectives, the implementation of legislation greatly varies across states.[3] The extent of state-mandated accounting, reporting, and auditing requirements (as of the mid 1970s) is presented in Exhibit 1.2. More than half of the states mandate some requirements. In addition, many states actively control and regulate financial practices of municipalities, such as specifying debt or tax limits, and these regulations may have an indirect impact on accounting, reporting, and auditing requirements.

Working within the state statutes, local governments establish and operate accounting systems by which to record, classify, summarize, and report transactions and events concerning their operations. Local governments have a tremendous amount of freedom in creating accounting systems (except where prescribed by state law), and this freedom is evident in the diversity found in practice. For the most part, municipal accounting systems are much less sophisticated than systems found in businesses having comparable revenues.[4] Furthermore, chief financial accounting officers earn substantially less in municipal employment than in corporate employment.[5] Disclosure quality may reflect any deficiencies inherent in accounting systems or management.

## Federal agencies

Most municipal governments receive funds from the federal government under one or more of many federal programs, such as general revenue sharing, Housing and Urban Development grants, Health and Human Services grants, and so on. The proportion of total municipal revenues for all cities in the United States derived from direct federal transfers grew from 11.6 percent in 1975 to 15.4 percent in 1979 (although some reduction is expected during the 1980s).

**Exhibit 1.2**
**Number of states mandating selected accounting,**
**reporting, and auditing requirements**

| Requirement | Number of States |
|---|---|
| Collect general financial data on municipalities | 39 |
| Use of standardized forms | 34 |
| Review data for supervision of general financial operations | 23 |
| Mandate accounting/auditing practices | 26 |

*Source:* J. Petersen, L. Cole, and M. Petrillo, *Watching and Counting* (National Conference of State Legislatures, Municipal Financial Officers Association, October 1977).

Additional federal funds flow to the cities through state intermediaries. Federal concern for municipal disclosures focuses on issues related to stewardship reporting, efficient operations of capital markets, and protection of federally chartered institutions.[6] Many federal programs prescribe particular accounting or auditing practices, and these are described in Office of Management and Budget circulars and in General Accounting Office Audit Standards.

**The Financial Accounting Standards Board**

The Financial Accounting Standards Board (FASB) is an independent, private sector, quasi-regulatory agency that promulgates financial accounting and reporting standards applicable to most business enterprises and many nonprofit organizations in the United States. The FASB derives its powers to establish reporting standards from the Securities and Exchange Commission (SEC), a federal regulatory agency created in the 1930s to oversee all activities related to the public securities markets, including the financial reporting practices of companies whose securities are traded on the various stock exchanges. Although the SEC has the legal power and practical authority to formulate accounting principles, it has delegated these rights to the FASB.

The FASB consists of seven full-time members with backgrounds in public accounting, industry, education, or government. The Board is supported by an extensive staff, which allows it to conduct research, evaluate alternatives, and hold public hearings to provide interested parties with due process. Thus the deliberations of the Board reflect broad-based input. Standards issued by the FASB are entitled *Statements of Financial Accounting Standards,* and these generally apply to specific types of transactions, for example, disclosure of pension information, capitalization of interest costs, or accounting for compensated absences. Statements of financial accounting standards are considered by most independent auditors and many municipal accountants as applicable to such governmental enterprises as public utilities, parking lots, and sports arenas. However, the mandate of the SEC to oversee securities markets does not extend to the municipal bond markets,[7] so the SEC has no authority over municipal accounting and reporting practices; thus the FASB has no delegated authority over municipal accounting issues.[8] [9]

## The American Institute of Certified Public Accountants

The American Institute of Certified Public Accountants (AICPA) is an association of over 160,000 certified public accountants, each of whom obtains the right to the professional designation, CPA, from a state board of accountancy. The AICPA promulgates standards of conduct for auditors, the auditing process, and the content of audit opinions. Through licensing and disciplinary actions, the state boards impose these standards on all CPAs. Auditing standards and Statements of Position (SOPs) are issued by the AICPA. The AICPA also issues audit guides that indicate to auditors peculiarities in particular industries. Of relevance in this discussion is the AICPA Audit Guide, *Audits of State and Local Governmental Units* (1974), as modified by SOP 80-2, which provides guidance on generally accepted accounting practices and auditing procedures for these entities. Other pronouncements of the AICPA specify accounting procedures applicable to governmental hospitals and governmental institutions of higher education. While AICPA audit guides establish mandatory standards for CPAs who audit governmental organizations, they also serve as guides to others who are not CPAs. The AICPA does recognize *Statement 1: Governmental Accounting and Financial Reporting Principles* (NCGA, 1979) as being authoritative literature describing preferred accounting practices.

## The National Council on Governmental Accounting

The National Council on Governmental Accounting (NCGA) is a quasi-regulatory agency established to promulgate professional standards for financial accounting practices for governmental organizations. The NCGA was established by the Municipal Finance Officers Association (MFOA), an organization of over six thousand individuals who are interested in establishing greater professionalism in the administration of the municipal finance function. The NCGA published *Governmental Accounting, Auditing, and Financial Reporting* (1968), which was widely recognized as the authoritative standard for municipal financial reporting until its replacement by Statement 1 in 1979. While it currently occupies a position somewhat parallel to the FASB, the NCGA is more limited in terms of staff and funding. Members of the NCGA serve on a part-time basis. The size of the research, support, and clerical staff reflects the limited funding available to the NCGA. The authority of the NCGA to enforce its accounting and reporting guidelines is limited. In addition, some states prescribe practices for municipalities that are not in conformity with NCGA pronouncements. Furthermore, many municipal financial statements are unaudited or are audited by persons other than CPAs (in contrast to business reports that are mostly audited by CPAs), so that the NCGA cannot use the AICPA to enforce conformance to Statement 1.

The variety of organizations involved in the oversight of governmental reporting naturally leads to variations in disclosure practices. However, a number of issues exist for which a general consensus of opinion in the institutional environment exists. These issues are discussed in the following section.

## CONSENSUS ON GOVERNMENTAL FINANCIAL REPORTING

No single authority dominates the specification of municipal accounting and reporting standards to the degree that the FASB dominates corporate reporting. Nevertheless, consensus has been achieved on several issues underlying key problems concerning the establishment of municipal financial accounting and reporting standards. Agreement exists about the financial accounting constituency and some of the purposes of financial reporting. This consensus provides a starting point for an examinatin of empirical evidence concerning the quality of current disclosures.

### Accounting constituency

Almost all authorities agree that governmental financial reporting must satisfy some of the information needs of the following parties: political participants, including boards of review, legislative bodies, and voters; revenue suppliers, including taxpayers, intergovernmental granting agencies, and paying consumers of governmnental goods and services; service beneficiaries; financial creditors, including bondholders and noteholders, banks, and others from whom governments borrow money; and employees, vendors, and other suppliers of goods or services. These constituencies may overlap, in that many taxpayers, service beneficiaries, and employees are also voters. Most authorities recognize that the information needs of these groups differ to some extent and that some priority might appropriately be granted to certain groups. Unfortunately, consensus has not been reached on the priority rankings of the different groups.[10]

These separate classes of external parties have a primary interest in the general purpose financial reports of governmental units. Governing bodies include councils and legislative authorities that are responsible for authorizing appropriations and taxes, for setting policy, and for overseeing the duties of management. These overseers need timely warning about situations that require corrective action. They also need information for establishing strategic and tactical policies, as well as for judging the efficiency and effectiveness of responsible officials. Creditors such as bondholders and prospective bondholders, vendors, and others who have extended credit are concerned with the probability that their loans will be repaid. Creditors look to the operating performance of the organization, its financial position, and its sources and uses of funds as indices of such probabilities of repayment. Local governmental units receive significant amounts of resources through transfer payments from other governmental units. Prospective resource providers need information about the nature and extent of the potential recipient's activities. Agencies with oversight functions, such as committees of the legislature or regulatory agencies, are authorized to exercise indirect control over governmental activities. Taxpayers, employees, and members of the general public round out the constituents of a governmental body. Individuals who belong to any one of these classes should have an interest in municipal financial reports.[11]

Despite consensus as to the appropriate constituencies, many questions about the information needs of these constituencies still need to be resolved, including the following:

1. Are the needs of users being satisfied?
2. Are the needs of different user groups similar?
3. What are the causes of disclosure deficiencies, if any exist?
4. What actions can be taken to reduce any existing disclosure deficiencies?

### Purposes of financial reporting

The central role of financial accounting information, as posited by the FASB (1980b, par. 22), is in helping users make decisions. Relevance and reliability have been identified as the two qualities that make accounting information useful to decision makers (par. 33).[12] Furthermore, the capacity of information to "make a difference" identifies it as relevant to a decision (par. 46). To be relevant, information must relate to at least one element of a decision model, such as an objective, a set of actions available to the decision maker, an outcome for each action, or a payoff for each outcome. In this sense, information is relevant according to how well it can help keep score, direct attention, and solve problems (Simon *et al.,* 1954); reveal expectations about payoffs and outcomes (Marshak, 1967); inform, instruct, and motivate (Ackoff, 1958); and clarify alternatives, indicate interactions, identify forces at work, and refresh memories (Mock, 1971).[13] The reliability of accounting information "rests on the faithfulness with which it represents what it purports to represent," that is, its representational faithfulness (FASB, 1980b, par. 59).

## Predictive ability

Three functions of financial reporting are accepted by most observers: predictive ability, representational faithfulness, and stewardship. As specified by the FASB (1980b, par. 47), the attribute of *relevance* obtains to a datum whenever it is "capable of making a difference in a decision by helping users to form predictions about the outcomes of past, present, and future events."[14] The predictive ability criterion has been well described in the literature since the mid 1960s,[15] and it has had a significant impact on accounting thought. In general, the criterion asserts that accounting measures that facilitate predictions about unknown events or states are relevant and that, *ceteris paribus,* greater (rather than lesser) predictability is desirable, whether measured in absolute or relative terms. A two-stage analysis is required in most applications of the criterion, the first to construct a predictive model and the second to evaluate the resulting predictions. The predictive ability criterion has been used in many empirical studies to assess the relevance of accounting data or procedures; for example, see Gonedes and Dopuch (1974) for a review and critique.

## Representational faithfulness

The representational faithfulness criterion has not been well articulated in the accounting literature, although it has been used, perhaps inadvertently, in empirical accounting research.[16] The FASB (1980b, par. 47, 49, 51) defines feedback value as an element of relevance, associated with the ability to confirm or alter prior expectations. This attribute may concern learning, memory, scorekeeping, and evaluation of model specification, and it may affect decisions through its effects on motivation, goal formation, and risk assessment. In a research setting, the feedback attribute implies that accounting measures are useful if they confirm historical events. The FASB (1980b, par. 59, 63, 64) also considers that decision usefulness is enhanced when accounting measures are reliable, in the sense that they represent what they purport to represent: "Representation faithfulness is closely related to what behavioral scientists call 'validity.' "

The relationship between feedback and representational faithfulness parallels the relationship between relevance and reliability. Ijiri and Jaedicke (1966) and McDonald (1967) described relevance and reliability in terms of two measurement properties, central tendency and dispersion, though they employed different terminology. Both studies described reliability as the distance between the mean accounting measure and the mean underlying "true" measure, where observations are obtained from samples drawn from unknown population distributions. Ijiri and Jaedicke termed the distance between means as "bias," while McDonald called it "displacement." The dispersion about the mean of accounting numbers was identified in both studies as being associated with reliability. Under this conception, reliability represents the confidence level with which a point estimate can be accepted as being representative of the accounting distribution.

From a measurement perspective, relevance and reliability coincide when a single measure of an accounting subject is well surrogated (e.g., "labor" is well surrogated by "labor costs") so that the strong correspondence between the two may be attributable to either relevance or reliability. When the object of scrutiny is a poorly surrogated accounting subject, for example, goodwill, the relationship between the relevance and reliability aspects of a single observation becomes less clear. However, both concepts can be united in a single empirical determination of the correspondence between an accounting measure and a known event or state. For example, accounting measures can be used as independent variables in multiple correlation or discriminant models, and the presence of a combined relevance and reliability attribute (of a point estimate) can be indicated by the amount of variation in the dependent variable "explained" by variation in the accounting measures. The distinction between feedback value and predictive value hinges upon prior knowledge of the decision outcome under consideration. Predictive value obtains when accounting measures help predict unknown outcomes with a larger than chance probability, while feedback value obtains whenever a significant correspondence is found between an accounting measure and an external phenomenon of known outcome, that is, when predictions are not required. Prediction implies a state "prior to complete knowledge,"[17] hence an "unknown" outcome. Predicting known outcomes is meaningless from a decision-making perspective. For example, predicting market returns of 1979 from earnings per share (EPS) data for 1980 is meaningless for investment purposes since the outcome is known. However, the feedback of 1980 EPS data in assessing 1979 market returns may confirm structural changes in an industry that were not evident in 1979 EPS data.[18] The distinction in use between feedback and predictive ability indicators parallels the distinction between lagging and leading econometric indicators.

## Stewardship

The stewardship function of accountability historically has been the dominant theme underlying the municipal financial reporting process. Stewardship responsibilities include the safekeeping and custody of organizational resources; compliance with all applicable statutes, contracts, and other legally binding covenants; and full and fair accountability for these custodial and compliance activities. Stewardship information provided through the accounting function may also facilitate the evaluation of municipal management's efficiency and effectiveness.

   The stewardship function traditionally has been discussed from the legal perspective of the master-servant relationship, or related to the legal duties of trustees. A few works have critically evaluated stewardship vis-à-vis other purposes of accounting. Rosenfield (1974) surveyed the literature on stewardship and concluded that steward-ship could be contrasted with other purposes in that it reflects past performance rather than future performance.[19]

A stewardship function is created whenever one person is engaged to work on behalf of others in a custodial or decision-making capacity. Hence stewardship involves the delegation of authority from a princi-pal to an agent and a commensurate assumption of responsibility by the agent. This agency relationship between municipal administra-tors and their constituents has been described in the accounting literature by Zimmerman (1977) in a significantly different way than the traditional view that concentrates on legal rights and duties. Modern agency theories presume that the agents (municipal adminis-trators) and the principals (constituents) are rational economic indi-viduals who attempt to maximize their own self-interests. Most often the self-interests of the administrators and constituents will differ. When this occurs, accounting disclosures serve as monitoring mecha-nisms that balance the conflicts of interest.[20] Advocates for the agency view of stewardship hold that information structured for stewardship purposes differs from information structured for decision-making purposes. (For further discussion, see Gjesdal, 1981.)

## MOVEMENT TOWARD CENTRALIZATION OF AUTHORITY FOR ACCOUNTING STANDARDS

Criticism of municipal accounting practice has been voiced now and then during the past century, but the frequency and vehemence of complaints reached epidemic proportions during the 1970s. While the immediate focus of attention in that decade concerned the fiscal plight of several large cities, much of the more reflective criticism considered the diffused institutional environment for establishing governmental accounting and reporting standards, as described above. Many critics claimed that the decentralized approach was neither efficient nor effective. Centralization of authority appeared to offer an opportunity for improving disclosure practices.

In 1980 representatives from several key organizations, including the FASB and NCGA, formed a committee to consider the formation of a Governmental Accounting Standards Board (GASB), which, if constituted, would promulgate financial accounting and reporting standards for governmental entities. In effect, the proposed GASB would assume control of powers presently decentralized among the public and private sector institutions described in this chapter. The committee members agreed that the proposed GASB should operate in the private sector, and several alternative organizational forms were considered. The committee devoted much attention to issues of jurisdiction, conflict resolution, independence, and costs. After much deliberation, the committee recommended in its final report (October 1981) that the GASB be organized as a parallel entity to the FASB. As envisioned, the GASB would establish financial accounting standards for state and local governmental entities, except for utilities, hospitals, universities, and other governmental entities that are similar to privately owned organizations. (Standards for these types of entities would be jointly established by the GASB and FASB.) Other aspects of the proposed GASB, such as number of members, relation to the Financial Accounting Foundation (a fund-raising, policymaking, and overseeing group), and an advisory council, would substantially parallel those of the FASB.

The Financial Accounting Foundation formed a committee to consider the formation of a GASB. As of this writing (March 1982), the committee has not reported the results of its deliberations, but many observers speculate that the report will be favorable and that eventually a GASB will be constituted.

In the meantime, the NCGA continues to issue statements of principle (most recently, number 3, *Defining the Governmental Reporting Entity).* Cooperation between the NCGA and the FASB appears to have increased, as is evidenced by the joint deferral of standards with regard to accounting for municipal defined benefit pension plans.

## SUMMARY

The diversity of views concerning appropriate disclosure practices for municipalities is traceable to the complexity of the environment in which the practices originate. The institutional environment for establishing reporting standards includes a variety of private and public sector organizations, each with its own particular perspectives and biases. The Financial Accounting Standards Board, the National Council on Governmental Accounting, and state and local authorities have promulgated standards for municipal financial reporting, while the American Institute of Certified Public Accountants and state and federal agencies provide guidance on auditing standards. Actions of other constituents also impact on disclosure practices.[21] Whether a Governmental Accounting Standards Board can eventually centralize authority for establishing standards remains to be seen.[22]

Municipal financial disclosure occurs within the framework established by the institutional environment, as described in this chapter. The remainder of this book will summarize the literature that empirically examines the quality of municipal disclosure.

## NOTES

1. Overlap may exist in the membership of these sectors, e.g., a city administrator may be a CPA, a member of the MFOA, and serve on committees of the FASB or NCGA.
2. The following list describes typical provisions of state law that are directed toward municipal disclosures:
   a) State supervision and assistance in the municipal budgeting process. Nearly all municipalities adopt a formal plan of financial operations embodying an estimate of proposed revenues and expenditures for a given fiscal period. State intervention may dictate the form, timing, and substance of the budgets. For example, state governments can check the budget for conformance with state laws governing levels of taxes or debts.
   b) State supervision and assistance in the municipal accounting function. States may be concerned with assembling a permanent record of financial activities by specifying the recording procedures to be used by municipal governments. A uniform chart of accounts may be specified for use by all municipalities of a given class within a state. Some states have subsidized the operations of nonprofit information-processing centers to computer process municipal accounting data through a standardized accounting system. Many states provide municipalities with a manual of accounting procedures.
   c) State supervision and assistance in the municipal financial function. Some states are concerned with the form or substance of financial

disclosures and hence prescribe a particular form for financial presentations and reports. Typical governmental disclosures are designed to demonstrate the correspondence between proposals in the budget plan and the actual results of operations. State governments may specify the type of funds for which financial reports must be prepared.

d) State supervision and assistance in the municipal audit function. States may be concerned with evaluating the legality and propriety of financial transactions, and hence they may mandate use of a specific system of authorizations or auditing procedures. Furthermore, states may specify auditing standards to assess the accuracy of disclosures or the conformity of accounting or reporting practices with prescribed standards. States may require audits of municipal reports at prescribed periods and by prescribed auditors, e.g., certified public accountants or state auditors.

3. Although each state has the legitimate power to regulate the accounting and reporting practices of its own municipalities, several organizations provide state administrators with opportunities to exchange ideas or present to others unified positions or consensus statements, e.g., the National Association of State Auditors, Comptrollers, and Treasurers; the Council of State Governments; the National Conference of State Legislatures; and the National Governors Association. The federal Advisory Commission on Intergovernmental Relations (ACIR) has drafted model legislation concerning regulation of municipal accounting practices, and several states have implemented legislation based upon the ACIR model.

4. While the fund and account group structure for governments appears to be more complex than the conventional corporate accounting structure, business systems also accommodate multiple subentities (subsidiaries) and intra-entity transactions. Furthermore, business systems are often designed to routinely generate cost accounting and control data, information that is rarely produced as an inherent function of most municipal accounting systems.

5. S. Smith examined compensation for matched samples of private and public sector employees (matched on the basis of age, education, and sex). During 1973 and 1975, males employed in state and local positions earned less than those in the private sector. See S. Smith, *Equal Pay in the Public Sector: Fact or Fancy,* (Princeton, N.J.: Princeton University Press, 1977) p. 68. Furthermore, examination of the "Employment Opportunities" columns in all 1981 issues of the *Newsletter of the Municipal Finance Officers Association* revealed no offerings for executive financial officers with six-digit salaries, amounts commonly paid for such positions in the private sector. Also see S. Langer, *The Accounting/*

*Financial Report (industry/government/education/non-profit),* 3rd ed. (Park Forest, Ill.: Abbott, Langer & Associates, 1982).

6. The following list describes some of the federal encroachments upon municipal accounting, reporting, and auditing options:

   a) Federal mandates to provide audited financial reports to specific federal agencies. Many federal grant programs require recipients to file specific financial statements with the granting agency at designated times. Furthermore, some of these reports must be audited by Certified Public Accountants, who comment upon the degree to which the financial statements conform with generally accepted accounting standards.

   b) Security market regulation specifies minimum disclosure requirements for approximately 20 percent of all new municipal debt offerings. Under a 1975 amendment to the Securities Exchange Act of 1934, underwriters for these debt issues are required to provide certain information to the public about offerings. The type of information demanded from municipalities is similar to (but less extensive than) the information demanded from corporate issuers of securities.

   c) Federally chartered commercial banks are subject to pressure from the Controller of the Currency and from the Federal Reserve System. These banks currently hold approximately 40 percent of all municipal debt securities. In an effort to "protect the public," these federal agencies could couple the acquisition of municipal securities with municipal disclosure requirements. For example, Senator Harrison A. Williams, ranking minority member of the Senate Banking Committee, introduced bills in 1979 and 1981 to mandate uniform state and local government accounting standards. These bills would require the creation of an Institute for State and Local Government Accounting and Financial Reporting designed to promulgate accounting and financial reporting standards applicable to state and local governments.

7. An amendment to the Securities Exchange Act in 1975 granted the SEC some control over municipal securities dealers.

8. However, other bodies such as the NCGA explicitly require governmental enterprises to adopt practices applicable to business operations.

9. The FASB does have additional powers delegated to it by the AICPA, which requires (through its code of ethics) members to conform to FASB standards.

10. For example, see MFOA (1981b) for a public comment on relative priorities of different constituencies and purposes.

11. See Anthony (1978), Holder (1980), and Drebin, Chan, and Ferguson (1981) for detailed discussions about the information needs of the several constituencies of municipal financial accounting.

12. General concurrence with this statement is found in the literature. For a review, see Mock (1976, pp. 96-104).
13. This list is intended to be representative, not exhaustive.
14. Some would question whether or not *predictions* apply to past events. However, predictions can be made about any event (past, present, or future) whose outcome is unknown.
15. See Beaver, Kennelly, and Voss (1968), Louderback (1971), and Greenball (1971) for an expanded discussion of this criterion.
16. The literature contains several empirical studies that purport to employ the predictive ability criterion in a research design that only contains the model-building stage; i.e., the evaluation of predicted outcomes is absent. These studies might appropriately be called feedback studies, in that they confirm the correspondence of variation in accounting measures and events of research interest.
17. See Kerlinger (1973, p. 459) for further discussion.
18. See Copeland and Ingram (1982a) for an empirical test of both the predictive and feedback functions of municipal accounting numbers with respect to changes in municipal bond ratings.
19. "As reports on accountable behavior, financial statements should contain information on past events. People are not accountable for the future, at least not until it arrives. Accounting standards used to prepare accountability reports should provide that they only report on the past" (Rosenfield, 1974, p. 129). Of course, this position had been noted previously. For example, May (1943, p. 20) states, "[For stewardship purposes] there is an attempt to appraise the past, and to measure the accumulative achievement to date; there is no attempt to use the past as a measure of the future."
20. The self-interests of both the administrator and the constituents depend upon their individual wealth and utility functions. To prevent the administrator from "enriching" himself or herself at the expense of the constituents, the constituents must either monitor the activities of the agent or devise alternative procedures to compensate for the deviations resulting when the administrator maximizes his or her self-interest at the expense of the constituents. Being rational, the constituents will take account of all available information and will use the information intelligently, in the sense that learning from past experience will prevent the recurrence of nonrandom mistakes; i.e., manipulation by the administrator will be discovered. Constituents will view accounting as one element in the total package used to control actions of the administrators. Accounting will be valued by the constituents as long as the relative cost-effectiveness of accounting as a monitoring device is lower than

that of other techniques. Being rational, administrators will recognize the tools available to the constituents to monitor and control the administrator's actions. Since the administrators have the ability to affect the cost of accounting as well as the choice of specific accounting, reporting, and auditing practices, they are motivated to demand specific practices that best present their perspectives.

21. Standard & Poor's bond rating agency has indicated that it will consider a failure to conform to generally accepted accounting principles as a negative factor in establishing a bond rating for a municipal bond issuer. See *Standard & Poor's Policy Statement: Municipal Accounting and Financial Reporting* (New York: Standard & Poor's Corporation, November 26, 1980).

22. Since state governments have the legal authority to specify municipal financial accounting and reporting standards, their concurrence with GASB standards is required before GASB standards will become widely accepted.

# Chapter Two

# THE QUALITY OF
# MUNICIPAL FINANCIAL DISCLOSURE

The quality of municipal financial disclosure has been a topic of much recent debate. Two questions have been raised: Exactly how good is the quality of municipal financial disclosure? and What are the determinants of quality reporting? Although a response to the first question introduces problems of measuring quality, an answer to the second question may provide suggestions for improving municipal disclosure quality; for example, once factors that influence quality are identified, improvements can be stimulated.

## MEASURING QUALITY OF DISCLOSURE

Measuring the quality of municipal financial disclosure requires an explicit definition of the word *quality*. Quality refers to a degree of excellence, as measured along a continuum from excellent to poor. This measurement can focus on three different dimensions that reflect the quality of municipal financial disclosure, as illustrated in Exhibit 2.1. At the highest level, quality can be measured with respect to decisions made by users of the financial reports, under the assumption (described in Chapter 1) that the ultimate purpose of financial reporting is to provide users with information useful in making decisions. Disclosures of excellent quality are very useful in making decisions, while disclosures of poor quality are less useful for decision-making purposes. Quality can also be measured with respect

**Exhibit 2.1**
**Focal point of quality measurements**

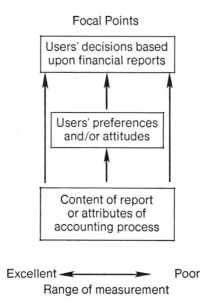

Focal Points

Users' decisions based
upon financial reports

Users' preferences
and/or attitudes

Content of report
or attributes of
accounting process

Excellent ◄————————► Poor
Range of measurement

to the preferences of the users of financial statements: full disclosure
of preferred data may be considered to be of excellent quality.
Attributes of the financial reports or the process by which data are
converted into financial reports can also be the focus of quality
measurements. This chapter describes research on the quality of
financial disclosures with respect to the accounting process and
users' preferences. The relationship between financial disclosure and
users' decisions is considered in the following chapters.

The three dimensions for measuring disclosure quality are not
independent. Attributes of the accounting process and the content of
financial reports may well affect users' attitudes and preferences, and
they undoubtedly affect the information set available for making
decisions. Users' attitudes and preferences probably influence their
decisions. (See Libby and Lewis, 1977, for evidence concerning the

interrelationships between these elements of human information-processing models.) Therefore, research on the quality of municipal disclosure must first consider accounting process attributes, since assumptions about the quality of financial data influence conclusions drawn from studies focusing on decision quality. For example, consider research that posits a relationship between voting decisions and accounting numbers or ratios: unless explicit controls are established, simple modeling of ratios and election outcomes implicitly assumes that all municipalities (1) use the same accounting procedures, (2) have identical charts of accounts, (3) maintain the same fund structures, and (4) aggregate data into the same financial statement classes. It also assumes that voters in all cities have the same demand for public goods and services and are equally capable and motivated to understand financial disclosures. An empirical finding of low correspondence between election outcomes (or any other decision variable from the attribute hierarchy) may reflect a "true" low correspondence, or it may indicate poor control for differences in users' preferences or financial disclosure content.

## QUALITY OF DISCLOSURE IN MUNICIPAL FINANCIAL STATEMENTS

Three extensive studies examined the quality of municipal financial statements: Cockrill et al. (1976) examined 44 municipal financial statements for fiscal periods ended in 1974; Ingram and Copeland (1981b) studied 55 municipal financial statements for fiscal periods ended in 1977; and Ernst & Whinney (1979) evaluated 100 fiscal 1977 reports. Each of these studies provided an indication of the quality and the diversity of municipal disclosures even though the studies differed in terms of sample size, sampling plan, and exact basis of comparison.[1] Conformance to generally accepted accounting procedures (GAAP) was considered the basis for making quality evaluations in all three studies.[2] The authors of all three studies concluded that the quality of the reports examined was, on the average, quite low. Details of these three studies follow.

## Basis for making quality evaluations

Authoritative reporting requirements for the period considered in these studies are specified in *Governmental Accounting, Auditing, and Financial Reporting* (GAAFR) (1968) and selected sections of *Accounting Research Bulletins, Accounting Principles Board Opinions,* and *Statements of Financial Accounting Standards.* The AICPA Audit Guide, *Audits of State and Local Governmental Units* (ASLGU) (1974), references and summarizes the major reporting requirements of these documents and therefore provides a useful synopsis of authoritative pronouncements. The Audit Guide became applicable for fiscal years beginning January 1, 1974, and prescribes GAAP in financial statements of state and local governments regardless of differences in legal requirements or local practices. Accordingly, the disclosures prescribed therein should be observed in external financial statements. (GAAFR, 1968, has been modified, subsequent to the period applicable to the three studies described below, by Statement 1, 1979, and Statement 3, 1982.)

Furthermore, Rule 203 of the AICPA Code of Ethics requires auditors to report material deviations from GAAP in financial statements that purport to present financial position and results of operations. Rule 203 applies to auditing in both the private and public sectors. Therefore the quality of disclosure in municipal financial statements reflects the manner in which the CPA profession demonstrates acceptance of its social role. Material deficiencies observed by the auditor should be corrected by the client or noted in the audit report.

Compliance with disclosure requirements in all three studies was determined by comparing the financial statements with the standards specified in the underlying authoritative statements of GAAP. Ingram and Copeland and Ernst & Whinney considered only those requirements that could be analyzed for compliance by inspection of the annual report. Compliance in the Cockrill *et al.* study was determined by reading the annual reports and then confirming the observations with municipal officers. Furthermore, Ingram and Copeland considered that noncompliance problems that were properly referenced in the audit report were adequately disclosed. Given these differences, care must be exercised in comparing the results of the three disclosure adequacy studies.

## Sample selection and scope

The Cockrill research team examined 44 fiscal 1974 annual reports for large cities selected under a nonrandom sampling plan. The authors imply that their findings may be biased, in that larger cities are assumed to follow better reporting practices than do smaller cities. Half of the sample was located in five states and may reflect state accounting, reporting, and auditing mandates.

Ingram and Copeland selected 55 audited annual reports for fiscal 1977, drawn at random from the municipalities listed in the *MFOA Membership Directory*. The populations of their sample ranged from 10,000 to 2 million, and the cities were selected from all geographical regions.

Ernst & Whinney examined 100 municipal annual reports with fiscal years ended in 1977. Cities included in the sample had populations ranging between 25,000 and 1 million, and represented 12 percent of all U.S. cities within these population ranges. The sample was biased toward larger cities, since the population for the sampled cities represented 22 percent of the population for all cities in the range class. The sample was geographically dispersed, and it included 39 percent of the cities included in the Cockrill *et al.* sample.

The scope of the Ernst & Whinney project was much broader than the other two. Ernst & Whinney developed a comprehensive guide designed to assist municipal financial managers in improving municipal financial disclosure practices. The guide presents tabulations reporting the frequency of particular disclosures found in practice, citations and source references to GAAP for these practices, and illustrations drawn from actual financial statements. In contrast, Ingram and Copeland were concerned with responsibilities of auditors to disclose deficiencies in their reports, and so they limited their examination to financial statements that had been audited by CPAs. (Eighty-four reports in the Ernst & Whinney sample were audited by CPAs, but Cockrill *et al.* do not report on this issue.)

## Adequacy of disclosure

Cockrill *et al.* focused on compliance with the 1974 requirements for 11 broad classes of information typically found in municipal financial statements. Each of the financial statements was examined to evaluate disclosure for each of the 11 topics, and any ambiguities were clarified by direct consultation with municipal officers. Tables were prepared to indicate the proportion of the total sample that was in compliance with specific disclosure requirements.

Compliance scores for 9 of the 11 categories studied by Cockrill *et al.* are summarized in the 1974 column of Exhibit 2.2. Major deficiencies were found in most categories. Only 7 percent of the reports complied with all pertinent reporting requirements for lease obligations, 16 percent disclosed accrued vacation and sick leave, and 24 percent disclosed the excess of vested pension benefits over accrued benefits. Disclosure compliance was higher in the remaining categories, but the level might still be considered low.

Compliance scores for these nine categories for the fiscal year 1977 are presented in the remaining column of Exhibit 2.2. Data were obtained from the Ernst & Whinney study.[3] Overall disclosure compliance remains low, but several noticeable differences appear, for example, disclosures of revenue sharing monies, special assessment activities, and pension disclosures. Undoubtedly, some of the differences reflect sample plan differences, in that the Ernst & Whinney study included many more small cities than were included in the Cockrill study. Ernst & Whinney reports on disclosure practices for cities arranged in size categories, and most of these exhibits indicate that larger cities provide more disclosure. However, many of the disclosure improvements from 1974 to 1977 probably reflect changing circumstances, such as the general financial credit tightening following the New York City bond default. Thus pensions, leases, and accrued vacation liabilities all reflect better disclosure in 1977 than in 1974, and these differences may well reflect changes in the state of the accounting art.

Exhibit 2.3 summarizes the principal results of the Ingram and Copeland study. The exhibit ranks the disclosure requirements from most to least adequate, references the AICPA Audit Guide for the disclosure requirements, and indicates the percentage of adequate

**Exhibit 2.2**
**Compliance with municipal reporting requirements**

| Disclosure Category | Percentage of Cities Complying | |
|---|---|---|
| | 1974 | 1977 |
| 1. Reporting date: report issued within 90 days after end of fiscal year | 39% | 38% |
| 2. Reported the following activities or balances: | | |
|     Revenue-sharing monies | 53 | 84 |
|     Intragovernmental monies | 65 | 57 |
|     Special assessment activities | 76 | 20 |
|     General purpose long-lived assets | 74 | 66 |
| 3. Overlapping debt disclosed | 50 | 35 |
| 4. Lease obligations fully disclosed | 7 | 12 |
| 5. Accrued vacation and sick leave | 16 | 38 |
| 6. Significant accounting policies (footnote disclosure) | 54 | 75 |
| 7. Pension disclosures: | | |
|     Excess of vested benefits over accruals | 24 | 41 |
|     Accounting policies used | 37 | 58 |
|     Funding policies used | 61 | 63 |
| 8. Basis of accounting: | | |
|     *Accrual or modified accrual* | | |
|         General funds | 83* | 77 |
|         Special revenue funds | 74 | 81 |
|         Debt service funds | 64 | 74 |
|     *Accrual basis* | | |
|         Capital projects funds | 63† | 52 |
|         Trust and agency funds | 62 | 46 |
|         Special assessment funds | 78 | 49 |
|         Intergovernmental service funds | 59 | 69 |
|         Enterprise funds | 77 | 77 |
| 9. Long-lived assets: | | |
|     Assets acquired and owned by entity | 74 | 66 |
|     Sources of funds used to acquire assets | 56 | 66 |

* Based on expenditures.
† Based on revenues.

*Sources:* Data for 1974 from R. Cockrill, M. Meyerson, J. Savage, E. Keller, and M. Maher, *Financial Disclosure Practices of the American Cities: A Public Report* (New York: Coopers & Lybrand, 1976). Data for 1977 from *How Cities Can Improve Their Financial Reporting* (Cleveland: Ernst & Whinney, 1979).

**Exhibit 2.3**
**Adequacy of disclosure in municipal financial statements**

| Rank | Disclosure Requirement | Ingram-Copeland Percent Adequate |
|---|---|---|
| 1 | Summary of accounting policies | 96% |
| 2 | Classification of revenues and expenditures | 95 |
| 3 | Comparison of revenues and expenditures with budget | 93 |
| 4 | Required bases of accounting | 91 |
| 5 | Separation of interfund receivables and payables | 87 |
| 6 | Terms and features of long-term debt | 85 |
| 7 | Required financial statements | 82 |
| 8 | Offsetting reserve for taxes receivable | 71 |
| 9-10 | Enterprise fund bonds disclosed as contingent liability | 68 |
| 9-10 | Year-end encumbrances | 68 |
| 11 | Principle of capitalization for fixed assets | 65 |
| 12 | Terms of revenue bond ordinance | 63 |
| 13 | Reserve for inventories | 62 |
| 14 | Lease arrangements and obligations | 60 |
| 15 | Use of asset valuation accounts | 58 |
| 16-17 | Actuarial reserves and liabilities of pension plans | 49 |
| 16-17 | Cost and market value of marketable securities | 49 |

*Note:* Results are for a national, random sample of 55 municipalities for fiscal years ended in 1976-77.

*Source:* Ingram and Copeland (1981b).

disclosures for the financial statements. All disclosures were not applicable to all statements, and in some cases the adequacy of the disclosure was not determinable from the information available. Ingram and Copeland conclude that the adequacy of disclosure appears to be a function of the visibility of the information in the financial statements. Disclosure items that are highly visible received higher rankings. For example, most statements reported a comparison of budgeted and actual revenues and appropriated and actual expenditures in accordance with GAAFR.

In contrast, disclosure items of low visibility were often inadequately reported. For example, the Audit Guide specifies that general obligation bonds to be repaid by enterprise funds should be reported as a contingent liability in a note to the statement of the general long-term debt group of accounts. This requirement was ignored in 32 percent of the statements that indicated the existence of this type of obligation.

Ingram and Copeland found 22 financial statements with unqualified audit reports, 28 with "except for" qualifications, 4 with "subject to" qualifications, and 1 with a disclaimer.[1] The percentage of qualifications is substantially larger than that for commercial enterprises. (*Accounting Trends and Techniques* reports that approximately 9 percent of the companies surveyed received "except for" qualifications in 1976.) The deficiencies noted were use of an inappropriate base of accounting, lack of required financial statements, and failure to record unfunded pension liabilities. Several unqualified reports referenced the omission of general fixed assets from the examination.

The percentages of inadequate disclosures in statements were analyzed by type of audit firm (national or regional/local) and by population size (greater or less than 150,000). These analyses revealed a large degree of consistency among subgroups. National firms audited 26 of the municipalities. Major deficiencies were observed in reporting pension liabilities, marketable securities, asset valuation amounts, reserves for inventories, and lease arrangements and obligations. Similar rankings and percentages were indicated by the 29 municipalities that were audited by regional and local firms.

The 38 smaller municipalities in the sample (less than 150,000 population) demonstrated primary deficiencies in reporting pension liabilities and the market value of marketable securities. The 17 larger municipalities demonstrated major deficiencies in reporting reserves for inventories and in use of asset valuation accounts. A lower percentage of inadequate reporting of pension liabilities (24 percent) was noted for the larger municipalities, in part because four audit reports referenced this deficiency. Given differences in determining "conformance," the results of the Ingram and Copeland study are not directly comparable to the findings of Ernst & Whinney. However, where comparison was possible, the results of the two studies were similar.

## Impact of diverse disclosure practices on cross-sectional comparisons

Without doubt, the quality of financial disclosures contained in financial statements will impact on the ability to perform meaningful cross-sectional comparisons of municipal operations. We shall briefly describe two studies that relate to this issue. Both studies were partially controlled for intervening variables by limiting sample selection to entities in one state and also by including limits on population size. Thus some degree of accounting practice homogeneity may have been expected to occur in the sampled cities.

Parry and Webster (1980) examined the effects of unrecognized long-term lease commitments on the debt balances of 18 cities in Pennsylvania. Using information obtained from each city's financial statements, Parry and Webster developed a composite measure of total debt by adding information about lease commitments (obtained from footnotes) to the amounts recognized as debt on the balance sheet or in the long-term debt group of accounts. Additional information about municipal lease commitments was obtained from the records of the Pennsylvania Department of Community Affairs. Of the 18 cities, 13 were found to have lease commitments that were not reflected in their financial statements. Three measures were developed to reflect the understatement of long-term liabilities: percentage increase in debt, increase in debt per capita, and percentage increase in debt service.[5] The high, low, and median of these three measures for the 13 cities with undisclosed lease commitments are presented below:

| Measure | High | Median | Low |
|---|---|---|---|
| Percent increase in debt | 940% | 76% | 3% |
| Dollar per capita increase in debt | $360 | $122 | $4 |
| Percent increase in debt service | 88% | 43% | 0% |

Without doubt, the unrecorded lease commitments have a material impact on these per capita and percentage measures. Parry and Webster also found dramatic shifts in the relative ranks of the 18 cities once unrecorded debt was considered.

Hansen (1977) considered methodological problems with inter-jurisdictional comparisons of municipal expenditure and revenue data by adjusting reported financial data to a common basis for three cities in New York State. Adjustments to reported data were made in consideration of six potential problem areas: differences in fund accounting systems; allocations of debt service, maintenance, and so forth; services purchased from contract agencies; substantive service differences grouped under common titles; city-county service alloca-tion differences; and method of funding indebtedness. Hansen views these adjustments as a vital first step that must be taken before evaluating whether or not one city spends considerably more for particular functional purposes than other cities. Hansen's research clearly indicates that a massive effort must be expended to obtain comparability but that significant differences will be found in the pre- and postadjustment functional amounts, and hence evaluations prob-ably will be affected by the adjustment process.

Both studies indicate the great difficulty of obtaining cross-sectional comparability based upon raw financial statement data. The underlying diversity of reporting practices is bound to affect users' opinions, and possibly even their decisions, to the extent that relative cross-sectional position serves as a basis of measurement.

## Comparison with business disclosure deficiencies

Are disclosure deficiencies more prevalent for audited municipal financial statements than for audited business financial statements? Ingram and Copeland (1981b) examined five previous research studies of corporate disclosure deficiencies; their findings are shown in

Exhibit 2.4. Four of these studies examined compliance practices for six Accounting Principles Board (APB) Opinions, and the fifth study was concerned with compliance with SEC *Accounting Series Release Number 138.* Compliance with APB Opinions 5, 8, 11, 12, 15, and 19 was evaluated by comparing the published disclosures contained in selected samples of annual reports with the "standards" suggested in the Opinions. Additional investigations were undertaken in studies 1, 2, and 5: the disclosure practice in question was cross-checked against SEC 10K disclosures in the first two studies, and follow-up correspondence requesting verification of findings was implemented in the last study. While the research underlying each of these five studies may be questioned, errors are likely to understate disclosure adequacy. In other words, the findings cited in Exhibit 2.4 probably represent the "worst case" disclosure. These findings provide a standard against which to evaluate municipal disclosure deficiencies.

Noncompliance with APB Standards ranged between 2 and 25 percent of sampled annual reports. APB Opinions 5 and 8 reflected greater noncompliance. Compliance with APB Opinions 12 and 19 each were evaluated in two independent studies, and similar levels of noncompliance were found. Ingram and Copeland (1981b) concluded that disclosure deficiencies in audited financial statements of business organizations occur to a greater extent than is commonly recognized, but, on the whole, to a smaller extent than found in municipal statements. Institutional forces, such as the SEC or the stock exchanges, may account for part of this difference. Other causes may arise from the municipal audit environment, such as audits performed by accountants other than CPAs and lower "penalties" for cities that issue qualified financial statements.

## MFOA Certificate of Conformance

The quality of municipal financial reporting has been measured for some cities by the Municipal Finance Officers Association (MFOA). Since 1945 the MFOA has issued a certificate to governmental units that publish an understandable comprehensive annual financial report covering all funds and financial transactions during the year. Requirements for obtaining a certificate go beyond those imposed by

Exhibit 2.4
Accounting deficiencies in business financial reports

| Study | Year | Compliance Item | Methodology/ Basis for Finding | Magnitude of Noncompliance |
|-------|------|-----------------|-------------------------------|----------------------------|
| 1 | 1973 | ASR* 138 | Compare 8K, 10K, and 10Q discrepancy in reporting Item 10(a) events | 63 out of 121 events<br><br>71 out of 127 events |
| 2 | 1972/3 | APB† 11 | Compare annual report and 10K | 18 obvious violators from 300<br>20 additional possible |
| 3 | 1969 | APB 12 | Compare annual report with disclosure requirements | 2 to 8 violators from 103 |
| 4 | 1971/2 | APB 19 | Compare annual report with disclosure requirements | Numerous instances of noncompliance over 20% |
| 5 | 1971 | APB 5<br>APB 12<br>APB 15<br>APB 19<br>APB 8 | Compare annual report with disclosure requirements | 25% noncompliance<br>7% noncompliance<br>4% noncompliance<br>5% noncompliance<br>12% noncompliance |

* Accounting Series Release
† Accounting Principles Board Opinion

*Source:* Ingram and Copeland (1981b).

*References*

1. A. J. Lurie and V. S. Pastena, "The Failure to Obey SEC Reporting Requirements: Compliance with ASR 138," *The Accounting Journal,* Winter 1977-1978, pp. 346-358.
2. J. R. Hasselback, "An Empirical Examination of Annual Report Presentation of the Corporate Income Tax Expense," *The Accounting Review,* April 1976, pp. 269-276.
3. T. G. Estes, "An Investigation of Compliance with and Desirability of Depreciation Disclosure Requirements in Accounting Principles Board

Exhibit 2.4 (cont.)

Opinion Number 12" (unpublished dissertation, University of Arkansas, 1971).

4. E. A. Spiller and R. L. Virgil, "Effectiveness of APB Opinion No. 19 in Improving Funds Reporting," *Journal of Accounting Research,* Spring 1974, pp. 112-142.

5. W. G. Grigsby, "An Evaluation of Selected Corporation Annual Reports for Compliance with Certain Recommendations of the American Institute of Certified Public Accountants" (unpublished dissertation, University of Oklahoma, 1973).

generally accepted accounting principles for governmental entities, applicable statutes, and regulations. The Certificate of Conformance is awarded by the MFOA to governmental units with financial reports that meet quite rigorous standards. These standards are summarized in a 32-page evaluation questionnaire. The MFOA provides a governmental unit with an extensive amount of reference material to provide preapplication guidance. To apply, a governmental unit submits five copies of its report to the MFOA within six months of its fiscal year-end. A review committee of the MFOA evaluates each submission, relative to MFOA standards (i.e., the review committee completes the 32-page questionnaire based on data in the annual report), and the committee's written conclusions contain suggestions for improvement in addition to a decision. Governmental units whose reports fail to win a certificate on first application are invited to resubmit in following years. In short, reports that earn a certificate have met technical standards of high quality.

As of September 1, 1980, 178 cities had financial reports that were awarded an MFOA certificate. Exhibit 2.5 indicates the number of states in which cities with certificates are located. In 19 states, no city had qualified for a certificate. The number of cities receiving certificates in the other 31 states varied from 1 to 36. Clearly, the distribution of cities with certificates indicating the high quality of financial reports is not uniform throughout the United States. Although not reflected in Exhibit 2.5, the distribution of cities with certificates is not proportional to the number of cities in each state

## Exhibit 2.5
## Distribution of MFOA certificates
## throughout the fifty United States, 1980

| Number of Cities with Certificate | Number of States | Total Number of Cities |
|---|---|---|
| 0 | 19 | 0 |
| 1 | 9 | 9 |
| 2 | 5 | 10 |
| 3 | 2 | 6 |
| 4 | 3 | 12 |
| 5 | 2 | 10 |
| 6 | 2 | 12 |
| 7 | 2 | 14 |
| 9 | 1 | 9 |
| 12 | 1 | 12 |
| 14 | 1 | 14 |
| 15 | 1 | 15 |
| 19 | 1 | 19 |
| 36 | 1 | 36 |
| Total | 50 | 178 |

Source: MFOA Newsletter, September 1980.

either. That is, quality of reporting (as measured by the MFOA) reflects a state effect. In some instances, state accounting, reporting, and auditing mandates represent causal factors leading to nonconformity with MFOA guidelines. For example, some states mandate the cash basis of accounting or auditing by state auditors, and either of these two provisions is sufficient to prevent the award of a certificate.[6]

## USERS' PREFERENCES AND ATTITUDES

One way to evaluate the quality of municipal financial disclosure is on the basis of the opinions of those persons who may use such data.

Although care must be exercised in generalizing from survey or questionnaire results, users' preferences, attitudes, and opinions can provide insight into a few of the issues raised in Chapter 1. Potential problems relating to naive interpretation of survey results are described in the next section. The section following that presents representative findings from survey research on financial disclosure quality. The concluding section describes methodological issues about multivariate analysis of users' opinions and municipal financial disclosure quality.

## Validity and reliability issues

Questions about the validity and reliability of empirical research on attitudes can focus on measurement scale, questionnaire design, sample selection, analysis of results, and interpretation of findings. With regard to scaling issues, users' opinions about specific disclosures can be measured in terms of nominal, ordinal, interval, or ratio values. The scale used in order to capture an opinion directly determines which measures of central tendency and dispersion are appropriately descriptive, and these in turn determine which statistical procedures should be used for evaluating the significance of differences between measures. For ordinally scaled responses, central tendency is measured by the median, dispersion is measured by the interquartile distance, and significant differences in central tendency can be measured by sign, runs, or Mann-Whitney $U$ tests and Kendall or Spearman rank correlations. The mean and standard deviation are appropriate descriptors of central tendency and dispersion for ratio-scaled responses, and student $t$-test, $F$-test, or Pearson product-moment correlation are appropriate statistical tools. Use of inappropriate descriptive measures or statistical procedures (relative to response scale) certainly must be considered in evaluating the findings reported in the literature. For further discussion of scale issues, see Mock (1976, p. 18ff).

The design of an instrument used to elicit opinions can have a major impact on empirical findings. First, the working of the stimulus might induce response bias or interpretative ambiguity. Questions about the quality of municipal financial disclosure can induce response bias or ambiguous response. Response bias occurs when the respondent provides an untrue response to enhance his own image or reacts to cues provided by the researcher. For example, a respondent may indicate that he does use a particular item of information even when he does not, simply because he thinks that he should be using that item. Consider the two italicized words in the following question. Which items of financial disclosure *do* you *use?* Respondents may react to the *do* as if it were *should, would,* or *could,* and they may respond to *use* as if it were *want* or *need.* Questionnaire design should be explicit enough to avoid such ambiguities or opportunities for response bias. Some questions should be repeated (possibly in an alternate form) to allow for reliability testing. (Questionnaire design is discussed in Oppenheim, 1966.)

Populations should be fully defined before sampling begins, keeping in mind that randomness in sampling underlies the validity of statistical testing. Unfortunately, user groups with clear-cut information needs are not well defined and easily accessible to researchers concerned with municipal accounting issues. Membership lists for such organizations as the MFOA or AICPA probably contain the names of many persons with low interest in issues about the quality of municipal financial disclosure. Sampling issues and nonresponse bias are discussed in Bachrack and Scoble (1967).

Grove and Savich (1979) describe factors that affect the reliability and validity of attitude research in accounting. Reliability concerns the consistency and stability of measurements, and validity relates to several issues, including content validity, criterion validity, and construct validity. Content validity involves the substantive and scale issues of each question and sample selection procedures designed to prevent bias. Criterion validity requires that all significant aspects of an attitude must be measured, including evaluations and emotions, beliefs and opinions, and action tendencies. Construct validity relates to the interpretation of results; in particular, generalizations from sample to population, from surrogate to principal, and from problem to solution. Dhaliwal (1980) identifies three sets of restrictive assumptions that inhibit generalizations from questionnaire findings to proscriptive actions: financial statement readers do not know which elements enter their decision models; the individual line items of most questionnaires are not independent; and economic conditions are not stable. Dhaliwal cities behavioral research that demonstrates that professional financial analysts have little insight into their actual decision-making processes. He also describes the effects of multicolinearity in evaluating opinions on disclosure quality, so that questionnaire responses to each line item incorrectly over-state values that could have been inferred from the presence of other related items. Changing economic conditions can affect the relative importance of specific items of information and hence opinions about disclosure quality.

### Representative findings on users' opinions

Although relatively few articles have been published that report the opinions of municipal financial statement users, some evidence does exist about four issues raised earlier in this book:

1. Are the needs of users being satisfied?
2. Are the needs of different user groups similar?
3. What are the causes of disclosure deficiencies?
4. What actions can reduce the problems?

Two articles provide some evidence of users' satisfaction. Boyette and Giroux (1978) attempted to determine the satisfaction of com-mercial bank officers who serve in investing or underwriting positions. They mailed a survey to all 106 commercial banks with assets exceeding $1 billion. Seven questions dealt with the perceived ade-quacy of presentations in financial statements. The usable responses from 45 banks indicated an overall dissatisfaction, based upon mean responses measured on a four-point scale (which was subsequently collapsed to two points).[7] Most of the perceived inadequacy con-cerned balance sheet disclosure, but on the average responding bankers indicated that presentations of the changes in fund balances and changes in financial resources were adequate. Although these general findings held across all of the banks, major differences were observed in responses grouped by bank size: in general, larger banks tended to rate the financial disclosures less adequate than did representatives of the smaller banks. Representative findings are presented in Exhibit 2.6.

**Exhibit 2.6**
**Perceived adequacy of municipal financial statements**

| Statement Attribute | Percent Adequate by Bank Size | | | |
| --- | --- | --- | --- | --- |
| | Over $5 Billion | $2 to $5 Billion | $1 to $2 Billion | All Banks |
| Comparison of budgeted with actual revenues and expenses | 31% | 43% | 42% | 39% |
| Disclosure of restricted assets | 39 | 36 | 21 | 30 |
| Disclosure of commitments and contingencies | 31 | 29 | 33 | 31 |
| Presentation of unissued bonds as an asset | 33 | 50 | 41 | 41 |
| Presentation of changes in fund balance | 46 | 71 | 72 | 64 |
| Presentation of changes in financial resources | 39 | 64 | 63 | 57 |
| Explanation of accounting policies | 31 | 46 | 37 | 38 |

*Source:* Boyette and Giroux (1978).

Maschmeyer and Van Daniker (1979) sought to determine the satisfaction of four groups of state financial statement users. Approximately four thousand questionnaires were mailed to officials in the executive and legislative branches of state government, representatives from the financial community, and members of various public interest groups. The overall response rate was 46 percent, but it ranged from a high of 72 percent for members of the executive branch to a low of 26 percent for representatives of the legislative branch. Responses to each question were measured on a four-point scale, but these were collapsed to two points in the published paper.

The overall satisfaction with local governmental financial reporting for the four groups ranged from a low of 51 percent to a high of 71 percent. In particular, members of the financial community consistently expressed concern about five aspects of financial reporting: a majority of financial community respondents were not satisfied with the timeliness, completeness, level of detail, ease of readability, and knowledge of what the figures represented. The next most critical group were representatives of the legislative branch, but their poor response rate precluded generalization. The majority of respondents from the other groups indicated satisfaction (averaging in the "somewhat satisfied" scale). See Exhibit 2.7 for an illustration of those findings.[8]

Luthy (1978) sought to determine the degree of correspondence between three groups of individuals who might evaluate municipal financial data to obtain information about a city's general obligation bonds. A 44-item questionnaire was mailed to 300 representatives from each of three groups: CPAs who were members of the MFOA, city finance directors, and bank officials from the 300 largest U.S. banks who had prime responsibility for investing in municipal securities. Response rates for the three groups varied between 55 percent and 61 percent. Consensus among groups was observed for only 10 of the 44 questions, and most of this consensus related to questions concerned with debt structure. Statistical analysis of the responses (on a five-point scale) included three sets of pairwise rank correlations and student $t$-tests for differences in group means (for standardized distributions).

Several authors used questionnaires in attempting to determine which actions would lead to improvements in municipal financial disclosure quality. These surveys tended to follow two different lines of inquiry. The first was concerned with the perceived usefulness or deficiency of selected items of financial disclosure. Respondents were asked to answer questions about (1) the *usefulness* of specific disclosures (see Boyette and Giroux, 1978; Maschmeyer and Van Daniker, 1979); (2) the *importance* of specific disclosures (see Boyette and Giroux, 1978; Luthy, 1978); (3) the *helpfulness* of disclosures (see Engstrom, 1978); and (4) the *satisfaction* with disclosures (see Maschmeyer and Van Daniker, 1979). A second approach elicited answers to questions that were more directly related to changes in

Exhibit 2.7
Percentage satisfied with aspects of local
government financial reports

|  | | Attribute | | |
| Subject | Overall Quality | Timeliness | Completeness | Detail |
| --- | --- | --- | --- | --- |
| Executives | 57% | 50% | 50% | 54% |
| Legislators | 51 | 53 | 48 | 48 |
| Financial analysts | 56 | 42 | 48 | 46 |
| Other | 62 | 54 | 58 | 59 |

*Source:* Maschmeyer and Van Daniker (1979).

disclosure practices. Respondents were asked to answer questions about (1) *suggestions for improvement* (see Maschmeyer and Van Daniker, 1979), (2) whether they *favor a change* (see Raman, 1981c), or (3) the *cause of a deficiency or effect of a change* (Copeland and Ingram, 1979). Three representative samples from this body of research will be briefly described in the following paragraphs.

Raman (1981c) examined the relative usefulness of municipal operating statements to municipal bond analysts and underwriters. A questionnaire was sent to 103 analysts and 194 underwriters, representing the population obtained from two mailing lists. Ninety-three percent of the analysts and 71 percent of the underwriters responded. Respondents were directed to indicate on a seven-point scale the degree to which they believed that each of nine suggestions for increasing the quality of municipal operating statements would improve disclosure. Raman transformed the responses from the seven-point scale to a two-point scale: *favor change* and *do not favor change.* Raman found few differences in the two groups of responses, at least as measured on the reduced dichotomous scale. Most positive was a suggestion that all items of revenue should be accrued (rather than recorded when cash is received), and respondents indicated the least concern for the accrual of actuarially determined pension costs (rather than cash payments for pension deposits).

Engstrom (1978) sought to determine the perceived information needs of municipal budget participants, including budget directors, chief executives, and city council members. In particular, Engstrom sought to determine preferences for selected items of information along a continuous Thurstone "incremental-rational" scale, anchored by the extremes of "line-item, object of case expenditure" and "full program" classes, with "full accrual" representing the midpoint. Items of financial information were reduced from 100 to 40, based upon pilot studies using municipal academic accountants as subjects. Nine hundred questionnaires were sent to the three types of respondents in 300 cities. On the average, 55 percent of the cities produced at least one response. Budget directors produced the highest response rate (49 percent) and council members produced the lowest rate (18 percent). Engstrom concluded that respondents would prefer to receive more information of a full accrual or program type than they are now receiving, even though they prefer to continue receiving the same level of departmentalized object expenditure data as is now available. Chief executives prefer to receive more program information than do budget directors. Engstrom concluded that the city officials perceive that the budgetary process would be improved if accounting systems were expanded to produce more full accrual and program data.

Copeland and Ingram (1979) surveyed 400 CPAs who were also members of the MFOA. Their opinions were solicited on whether each of 14 possible reasons for deficient disclosure practices were "not a cause" or were a "major cause," using a five-point scale. Respondents were also asked to rate the potential for improving disclosure practices of eight actions. The response rate on the initial mailing equaled 42 percent, and these findings are reproduced in Exhibits 2.8 and 2.9. In the opinion of the respondents, the primary causes of the disclosure deficiencies were auditor and client knowledge of governmental accounting principles and auditor and client incentives to comply with these principles. These responses suggest that both educational and regulatory problems exist within the profession, and institutional problems related to the specification of

**Exhibit 2.8**
**Causes of disclosure deficiencies**

| Rank | Cause | Mean Response |
|---|---|---|
| 1-2 | The auditor was not sufficiently knowledgeable of GAAP for governmental units | 3.59 |
| 1-2 | Insufficient knowledge of accounting matters on the part of the municipal client | 3.59 |
| 3 | Insufficient incentives to encourage client to conform with GAAP | 3.50 |
| 4 | The auditor was insufficiently motivated to carefully monitor conformity with GAAP | 3.29 |
| 5 | Inadequate accounting system maintained by client | 3.17* |
| 6 | Ambiguities within GAAP for governmental units | 2.83* |
| 7 | Inadequate attention was given by the auditor to reviewing financial statements | 2.79* |
| 8 | Conflicts between local preferences or conventions and GAAP | 2.78* |
| 9 | Conflicts between legal requirements and GAAP | 2.73* |
| 10 | Audit procedures, as reflected in the working papers, were deficient | 2.67 |
| 11 | Audit planning and supervision were deficient | 2.61 |
| 12 | Insufficient cooperation by client | 2.61 |
| 13 | The auditor and client disagreed over the applicability of GAAP | 2.15 |
| 14 | Conflicts between GAAFR and AICPA Audit Guide | 2.03 |

*Responses demonstrated a lack of consensus on these items. 1 = not a cause; 5 = major cause.

*Note:* Results are from a national sample of 157 CPAs who engaged in municipal audits during the 12-month period ended in November 1978.

*Source:* Copeland and Ingram (1979).

**Exhibit 2.9**
**Corrective action to improve**
**municipal reporting**

| Rank | Action | Mean Response |
|------|--------|---------------|
| 1 | The development of a concise uniform set of accounting standards for governmental units | 4.06 |
| 2 | Increasing the municipal audit fee schedule to a level comparable with commercial audit fees | 3.80 |
| 3 | The development of a conceptual framework for governmental financial accounting | 3.74 |
| 4 | Increasing the sanctions against CPAs who perform deficient municipal audits or fail to qualify opinions when municipal financial statements are deficient | 3.68 |
| 5 | Increased attention to continuing education of auditors | 3.59 |
| 6 | Greater peer review of municipal audit working papers and procedures | 3.35 |
| 7 | Required registration of municipal securities with the SEC | 2.84* |
| 8 | Transferring the responsibility for the establishment of governmental accounting standards to the FASB | 2.81* |

*Responses demonstrated a lack of consensus on these items. 1 = no improvement; 5 = major improvement.

*Note:* Reponses are from a national sample of 157 CPAs who engaged in municipal audits during the 12-month period ended in November 1978.

*Source:* Copeland and Ingram (1979).

accounting principles also exist. Concerning possible corrective actions, the four most potentially fruitful solutions are increasing audit fees, increasing sanctions for deficient performance, developing concise standards, and developing a conceptual framework. These two sets of responses were consistent, in that causes can be linked with corrective actions. Institutional and professional changes that would improve comprehension of accounting principles and auditor incentives were viewed as being effective by the majority of respondents. More drastic changes, such as transferring full responsibility for establishing governmental accounting principles to the FASB or requiring registration of municipal securities with the SEC, received mixed responses.

Taken at face value, these studies can provide tentative answers to the four questions raised earlier in this chapter. First, it appears that most of the information needs of diverse groups of "users," as surrogated by respondents to questionnaires, are not being satisfied. Furthermore, the perceived needs for information differ across the groups, and may even differ within the groups, given such intervening factors as size of the institution. Given these differences of perceived disclosure differences between and within groups, it is not at all surprising that no one single cause has been identified, and so no simple solution is available. However, several possibilities for working toward a solution may be elicited through survey and questionnaire research.

Taken at less than face value, all of the findings are potentially subject to the problems described in the preceding section. Note, however, that several of the authors properly recognized the potential problems and appropriately qualified their conclusions or modified their procedures.

## Multivariate analysis of users' opinions and disclosure quality

Ingram and Copeland (1979) developed linked bivariate models of users' opinions by correlating responses (using Spearman's rank correlation) to each line item of their questionnaire to the responses for the other line items, over all 157 respondents. Zero order correlation coefficients indicated the strength of linkages between responses for each pair of questions. None of the four major cause factors were directly linked to the four most fruitful solutions. Other expected relationships failed to materialize; for example, auditor knowledge was not linked directly to increased continuing education. However, other interesting interactions were revealed; for example, audit procedures were directly linked to peer review and increased sanctions, but audit fees were only linked to increased sanctions. The strongest bivariate relationships were found between the following pairs: audit planning and audit procedures; concise standards and conceptual framework; and audit planning and financial statement review. All findings appeared to have face validity.[9]

Other researchers concerned with users' opinions of disclosure quality (including Engstrom, 1978) have developed multivariate models. Path analysis is one technique used in the social science literature that may be applicable to modeling opinions on disclosure.[10]

## DETERMINANTS OF DISCLOSURE QUALITY

Several researchers have attempted to identify the determinants of corporate disclosure quality, including Cerf (1961), Singhvi and Desai (1971), Buzby (1974), and Firth (1979). Determinants of the quality of municipal disclosure have been studied by Zimmerman (1977), Baron (1978), Engstrom (1978), and Copeland, Ingram, and Magann (1981). While the model underlying some of these research efforts was unspecified, all of the efforts can be considered in terms of the following model:

$$\text{Disclosure quality} = f \left( \begin{array}{cccc} \text{Internal} & \text{Internal} & \text{External} & \text{Interaction} \\ \text{need,} & \text{ability,} & \text{constraints,} & \text{effects} \end{array} \right)$$

All of the corporate studies cited above developed a compound disclosure index for a dependent variable by summing the products of the perceived importance of a disclosure and the extent of disclosure, for example,

$$\text{Compound index } = \Sigma \text{ (Importance of disclosure}_j$$
$$\times \text{ Extent of disclosure}_j)$$

Although this compound index approach may have some promise for studying municipal disclosure, it has not been applied to date (see Dhaliwal, 1980, for a critique). Instead, the dependent variable in much research on determinants of municipal disclosure concerned selected elements of the index (i.e., either measures of importance or extent). Measures of importance were obtained by questionnaire (Engstrom), while measures of extent were variously measured as number of reports issued, when issued, and to whom issued (Baron), number of pages and number of exhibits (Zimmerman; Copeland, Ingram, and Magann), and timing and Certificate of Conformance awards (Copeland, Ingram, and Magann).

Several of these studies examined *a priori* reasons for disclosure quality differences. Administrators in some cities *need* more or better information in order to manage their operations than do administrators in other cities, due to differences in the complexity of operations and inherent risks or uncertainties. Complexity of operations should be a major determinant of the need for information. More information is needed in order for administrators to manage complex organizations than is needed for simple operations. Complexity, in turn, is a function of the size of the city, the number of municipal functions provided by the city, the number of municipal employees needed to perform these functions, and the organizational structure of the city. The size of the city can impact on complexity of operations both in terms of the number of citizens served (population) and in terms of the population density. Several different types of threats can be linked to the need for more information. Financial distress, as measured by the degree of imbalance between revenues and expenditures, presents a clear-cut threat to municipal operations that necessitates increased surveillance of municipal operations. Sudden increases in unemployment, crime, or poverty present threats to cities as administrators attempt to marshal resources to combat these problems. Organization size was considered in all of the eight research studies cited above. Furthermore, Baron and Copeland,

Ingram, and Magann employed bond ratings (a measure of financial risk) as second surrogates for "needs for information."

Administrators in some cities have the ability to obtain and use more or better information than those in other cities. Such factors as the education and experience of the administrators and the quality of the information-processing system affect the ability of administrators to use financial information. Engstrom measured *internal ability* as the educational level and years of experience of administrators and the availability of data.

Constraints may be placed on the accounting and reporting options of a given city by parties external to the local management. Furthermore, these constraints may be legally binding or economically within the self-interest of the city. Chief among the legally binding constraints are state-mandated accounting, reporting, and auditing requirements; federal reporting and auditing requirements; and contractual reporting requirements. State-mandated accounting, reporting, and auditing requirements vary from state to state. Since municipal governments are created under state law, state governments do have the right to impose such requirements on local governments. Some states make full use of these rights by requiring municipalities to employ a state-designed uniform accounting system, specifying a standardized reporting format, and designating audit requirements. Other states have made little use of their ability to specify local accounting, reporting, or auditing standards. For example, South Carolina has imposed no such requirements on its municipal governments. The incidence of state mandates (as of 1976) is summarized in Exhibit 2.10.

Contractual reporting and auditing requirements are typically created when the city enters into an agreement with a third party and the agreement is formalized into a contract. For example, bank loans, bond covenants, or agreements with bond rating agencies are all formalized by contract, and all may require the city to provide certain types of information, and in some cases, to have an auditor attest to the conformity of that information with specified standards. External constraints were specified in the research literature by the degree of state control (Engstrom; Copeland, Ingram, and Magann), type of audit (Baron; Copeland, Ingram, and Magann), and political environment (Baron; Zimmerman; Copeland, Ingram, and Magann).

**Exhibit 2.10**
**Number of states mandating selected accounting,**
**reporting, and auditing requirements**

| Requirement | Number of States |
|---|---|
| Collect general financial data on municipalities | 39 |
| Use of standard forms | 34 |
| Review data for supervision of general financial operations | 23 |
| Mandate accounting/auditing practices | 26 |

*Source:* J. Peterson, L. Cole, and M. Petrillo, *Watching and Counting* (National Conference of State Legislatures, Municipal Financial Officers Association, October 1977).

The empirical results of all of these studies must be considered tentative at best.

## SUMMARY

This chapter has examined two dimensions of municipal disclosure quality: the deviation between actual reporting practices and explicit standards, and the opinions of various user groups concerning their perceptions about the quality of municipal disclosures. Empirical studies have documented the pervasive noncompliance of municipal reports with generally accepted accounting principles for governmental entities. Most surveys of users indicate that users are not fully satisfied with contemporary disclosures. Most of the research cited in this chapter supports the contention that current disclosure practices are "deficient" for many jurisdictions. A number of suggestions for correcting reporting problems were examined.

Note, however, that the empirical research on municipal disclosure quality is of recent origin (although anecdotal evidence on the poor quality of disclosure has been reported for the past century[11]). Most of the references cited in this chapter have been published since the mid 1970s, and the pace of such publications is on the increase. Replications and original studies on each of the issues we have described are becoming available, and some of the new findings probably will contradict those reported here.

Even though evidence from additional replications is not currently available, some implications from the research findings appear to hold:

1. Survey results suggest that different constituents have different perceived needs for information: one information set is unlikely to satisfy the needs of all constituents.

2. Even within a particular constituency group such as investment bankers, subgroups appear to desire different data sets: one information set is unlikely to satisfy all members of a given constituency.

3. Financial statements in many jurisdictions employ practices that are not in conformity with GAAP: a modification of GAAP in order to improve disclosure quality may not be effective unless the change is sufficient to induce municipal officers to conform to the modified GAAP.

4. Although qualified audit opinions do, in many instances, indicate nonconformance with GAAP, many instances of noncompliance occur without an accompanying qualification: a modification of GAAP may not be sufficient to encourage auditors to write opinions that better reflect actual disclosure practices.

The next chapters of this book consider the usefulness of municipal financial reports from the perspective of actual decision making. Empirical research is summarized that describes the usefulness of this information for making voting decisions (Chapter 3) and investment decisions (Chapter 4). This research extends beyond questions of technical compliance and beyond opinions of usefulness: it identifies how information may actually be employed in various decision contexts.

# NOTES

1. A fourth study by Haseman and Strauss (1981) also bears on the issue. Fiscal 1978-79 annual reports were examined for 122 cities in order to measure the variance between actual accounting and reporting practices and those prescribed by GAAP. This excellent study is similar to the three described in this chapter, and it certainly should be examined by those interested in undertaking related research.

2. Measuring deviations between GAAP and actual reporting practices does not necessarily imply that the GAAP standards reflect optimal representations. The deviations merely measure the degree of compliance. Some observers believe that municipal GAAP are suboptimal and that reports that are in noncompliance may actually be of better quality than those in compliance. Although this outcome is possible, it does not occur with high frequency. Current efforts to improve the quality of municipal disclosure tend to be evolutionary (e.g., NCGA Statement 3) rather than revolutionary.

3. Given the ambiguities of the Cockrill classification criteria, we may have mismatched some of the Ernst & Whinney data. We assume responsibility for any mismeasurements.

4. Of the 84 reports audited by a CPA described in Ernst & Whinney (1979), 26 percent had unqualified opinions on all funds. Most qualifications were found for the general fixed asset group (50%) and for the enterprise fund (35%).

5. Parry (1982a) extended this study to consider the impact of capitalizing lease costs on nine financial ratios, with similar results.

6. Evans and Patton (1981) sought to identify the determinants of voluntary participation of cities in the MFOA Certificate of Conformance program. Multiple regression and probit models were used to measure the relationship between the propensity of a city to participate in the program and several attributes of the city and its management. Cities that have more debt, higher quality management, professionally active officers, and a manager form of government are more likely to participate in the program. Although the best model only explained less than 20 percent of the variation in participation, all variables except debt were significant at the .05 level for a sample of cities falling within a limited population range.

7. Measuring the importance of 21 financial disclosures on a 1-to-4 response scale may obscure the "true" weight of importance ascribed by bankers to each disclosure. Howard and Johnson (1981) were so con-

cerned with this potential problem that they replicated the study of Boyette and Giroux, except that they substituted magnitude scaling as a measure of responses. Using magnitude scaling, survey participants who believe that tax rate limits are five times more important than bond ratings can assign it this weight. A relatively high .734 Spearman rank correlation existed between the two ranking, implying that the two scales provide similar results.

8. Further analysis and interpretation of the survey data resulted in the production of a book-length exposure draft of a research report: R. Van Daniker and K. Pohlmann, *Preferred Accounting Practices for State Governments* (Chicago: NCGA, 1981).

9. To better consider all interrelationships within the sets of "causation question responses" and "corrective action question responses," Ingram and Copeland used principal components factor analysis to identify subsets of responses representing broader themes. The factor analysis also developed weights for the contribution of each question response to each theme. Three "causative" themes and three "corrective" themes were identified, and the interrelationships between the two sets of themes were evaluated by use of canonical correlation. Although the results of the factor and canonical analyses were statistically significant, Ingram and Copeland focused their attention on the methodological innovation for future research on disclosure (rather than for the findings). They concluded that research on multivariate linkages between municipal attributes, auditor attributes, and institutional attributes should prove fruitful.

10. For example, see H. Asher, *Causal Modeling* (Beverly Hills, Calif.: Sage, 1976).

11. Zimmerman (1977, p. 107) quotes one such observation dating to 1898.

*Chapter Three*

# THE UTILITY OF
# ACCOUNTING INFORMATION
# FOR VOTING DECISIONS

As indicated in Chapter 1, most public statements about the objectives of financial reporting by governmental entities identify voters as a potential beneficiary of accounting information. For example, the American Accounting Association Committee on Accounting in the Public Sector (AAA Committee, 1977) posited that the basic objective of governmental accounting is "to provide information on which constituents can base a decision to retain or replace the incumbent." The purpose of this chapter is to review the theoretical and empirical literature on voting and voter behavior as phenomena to be influenced by accounting information.

## ASSUMED LINKAGES BETWEEN ACCOUNTING AND
## ELECTION RESULTS

The linkage between accounting information and voters' decisions rests on the assumptions that municipal accounting numbers reflect the economic consequences of incumbent administrators' political choices and that a dominant faction of voters impound these numbers in the election process (AAA Committee, 1977, pp. 38-43). Thus economic awareness and rationality on the part of voters and politicians are preconditions to the utility of accounting information for voting decisions.[1]

55

These assumptions are consistent with the economic theory of public finance and the investor theory of voting addressed in the economic and political science literatures. The economic theory of public finance (popularized by Downs, 1957) is based upon rational behavior by voters and politicians consistent with their own economic self-interest. The voting process is recognized as a mechanism through which individuals register their desires for public goods. The mechanism functions to specify the amount and mix of goods and services to be provided by the government (AAA Committee assumptions 1 and 2). In order to obtain office, politicians must promise to implement policies that result in a mix of expenditures and taxes (or charges) appealing to a dominant coalition of voters (AAA Committee assumption 3).

The voter is also perceived as being economically rational, with the vote representing an investment in a specific mix of collective goods. The election process is a means by which voters select the political administrator who is perceived to be most consistent with the voters' utility functions. The implications for voter behavior are clear if one assumes an environment of perfect knowledge, costless information, and homogeneous classes of voters. Each class of voters would evaluate each candidate as follows:

$$E(U_j) = \Sigma W_i A_{ij}, \tag{1}$$

where $E(U_j)$ is the expected utility of candidate $j$, $W_i$ is the weight ascribed to the $i$th attribute, and $A_{ij}$ is the perceived value of attribute $i$ for candidate $j$ (AAA Committee assumption 4). Each class would then maximize the expected utility function. Expected utility is thus a function of candidate attributes and voter predispositions. Candidates would, of course, attempt to maximize their vote by assessing voter predispositions and addressing themselves to these predispositions so as to maximize the utility function of a dominant coalition.

The role of accounting in this environment would depend on the extent to which accounting numbers capture information relevant to the attributes of concern to voters. Since it is assumed that voters are motivated by economic self-interest, an accounting system that reports on such economic issues is consistent with voter concerns

(AAA Committee assumption 5). To the extent that the accounting system reflects the mix of expenditures and taxes to be expected from each candidate, the system could play a significant role in the election process (consistent with the AAA Committee position). These relationships are illustrated in Exhibit 3.1. Rational politicians will make political decisions that will facilitate reelection; the consequences of these decisions will be reflected in the accounting reports; and rational voters with homogeneous expectations will base their election decisions on the costless and certain information provided by the accounting system[2] (see Exhibit 3.1).

Considering another aspect of economic rationality, Tiebout (1956) posited that fully mobile individuals will move to the city where their preference patterns for public goods and services are best satisfied. These individuals are assumed to have full knowledge of differences among revenue and expenditure patterns and to react to these differences as rational, utility-maximizing decision makers. Under Tiebout's theory, different cities will offer different packages of public goods and services and the voting population of each city will prefer the package that is offered by that city.

## EVIDENCE ON RATIONALITY

The formulation of the function of accounting in the public sector described above would require evidence on only two propositions to lead to a meaningful objective: (1) voters and politicians demonstrate rationality consistent with utilitarian marginalism, and (2) economic information reflects attributes consistent with rational decision making. Evidence exists on both counts.

### Voter and politician rationality

Davis and Hinich (1966) specified a functional relationship between voting and perceived candidate attributes that postulated voter rationality, as follows:

$$L_N = (X_i - \theta_i)' \, A_i (X_i - \theta_i), \qquad (2)$$

**Exhibit 3.1**
**Costless, certain accounting information and**
**election decisions of homogeneous voters**

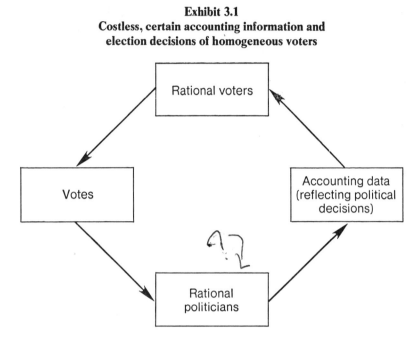

where $L_N$ is an individual voter's loss function for candidate $N$, $X_i$ is a vector of $i$ candidate attributes of concern to the voter, $\theta_i$ is a vector of perceived candidate positions on the $i$ attributes, and $A_i$ is a positive, semidefinite saliency matrix expressing the voter's assessed weights of the $i$ attributes. A voter would attempt to minimize $L$ and vote for the corresponding candidate. Shapiro (1969) tested voter rationality based on the Davis-Hinich functional relationship by surveying a sample of voters who specified individual assessments of attributes they considered important and of candidate qualifications based on those attributes. The loss function successfully predicted 85.5 percent of the sample vote in the 1968 presidential election.

Voter rationality in school budget elections was studied by Hall and Piele (1974), who attempted to forecast individual voter decisions. They found that voters make decisions consistent with economic self-interest. Variables of significance in the decision-making process were parental status, age, and home ownership. Voters with school-aged children and voters with children nearing school age were more likely to vote in favor of budget increases. Otherwise, prospective increases in property taxes were a negative factor affecting home owners.

It is consistent with economic rationality to assume that voters will desire to consume more of a public good the smaller the part of the bill the voters have to pay. The Hall and Piele study also found that socioeconomic status was an important determinant in voting decisions, as voters of higher socioeconomic status were likely not to support service increases that significantly impacted their tax burdens. The most important indicator of current voting behavior discovered in this research was past voting behavior, indicating voters are consistent in their assessments of self-interest over time.

Evidence also exists to indicate that politicians are aware of voter economic rationality and are themselves conscious of voter choice implications in policy decisions. For example, Davis and Haines (1966) studied the association between indicators of voter preferences and expenditure decisions in municipalities. They assumed that the indicators reflected the self-interest of dominant voter coalitions and that politicians would respond to these indicators in making policy decisions in order to appeal to a majority of their constituency. They found a significant association between independent variables used as indicators of voter preferences—population density, percentage of owner-occupied housing, and median family income—and expenditure policies in the areas of general government, public safety, health and sanitation, streets and highways, and interest on public debt.

Similar associations were reported in extensive studies by Dye (1966), who linked socioeconomic development variables such as urbanization, industrialization, income, and education with policy variables—expenditure and tax decisions. Dye investigated congressional elections across 50 states. The results suggest that politicians behave as though voters make decisions in accordance with economic self-interest and therefore politicians make policy decisions that are in accordance with their own self-interest (to help them be reelected). In effect, politicians use taxing and spending programs to acquire votes. By designing a program to redistribute costs and services, a politician can appeal to uncommitted voters or to voters committed to his or her opposition. Tufte (1975) found that the federal government frequently engages in economy-expanding activities during election years that it does not engage in during nonelection years.

### Economic variables

Are economic variables significant elements in voter decision models? Some evidence has been reported that links voting results to specific economic conditions.

Most research into the impact of economic factors on voting decisions has occurred at the presidential election level. Kramer (1971) used multivariate regression to demonstrate that declining real income reduces the vote for the party of the incumbent president, whereas rising real income increases the vote. However, Stigler (1973) produced results that refuted Kramer's, and Arcelus and Meltzer (1975) concluded that economic conditions do not affect voting decisions.

Bloom and Price (1975) explained the negative results obtained by Stigler and by Arcelus and Meltzer by introducing asymmetry into the economic conditions. They posited, as did Campbell *et al.* (1960), that changes in political party balance are induced primarily by negative rather than positive attitudes toward the incumbent party. Their findings demonstrated that short-run economic downturns, as revealed by percentage changes in real per capita personal income, reduced the vote for the incumbent president but that an upturn produced no substantial effect. These results indicated a "throw the rascals out" phenomenon. They also found that economic events occurring in the year before the election were most critical.

Meltzer and Vellrath (1975) also found that economic variables, including the level of services (and costs) specified as policy decisions and aggregate performance variables, such as unemployment and inflation, affected presidential elections. These researchers found that the importance of different variables changed across elections, and the researchers concluded that they could not develop a predictive theory of voting behavior.

Other research also supports (with some exceptions) voter concern for economic conditions. Tufte (1975) concluded that a change of $100 in real disposable per capita income was associated with a national change of 3.5 percent in midterm votes for congressional candidates of the political party represented by the president. Fiorina (1978) concluded that a voter's personal economic condition affects his or her presidential vote. However, he also concluded that the evidence was not as strong for on-year congressional elections and that economic conditions probably did not strongly influence midterm congressional elections.

Many tests of the Tiebout theory confirm differences in preference patterns across constituents and differences in service packages across cities (e.g., see Oates, 1969, and Cebula, 1974; Raman, 1979, discusses some implications of the theory for accounting). Researchers have examined the association between city finances and socio-demographics.[3] Liebert (1974) undertook an extensive examination of the differences among cities and demonstrated that such differences do exist. Fabricant (1952) identified three variables—per capita income, population density, and percent urbanization—as being highly correlated with differences in expenditures. Sacks and Harris (1964) and Bahl and Saunders (1965, 1966) reexamined Fabricant's findings and also concluded that there was a high correlation between expenditures and socio-demographic characteristics. Among the variables used by researchers to explain differences in expenditures are population density, percentage of nonwhite population, population age, per capita income, percent of population below poverty level, percent of housing occupied (or similar housing variables), retail sales revenue per capita, percent of population employed in manufacturing, and other occupational decomposition variables.

## Implications

The implications for accounting of the research cited above are consistent with the reasoning of the AAA Committee. Voting choices are made by rational decision makers who attempt to maximize the utility obtained from a given election result. Politicians are aware of voter decision processes and make policy decisions that will appeal to a dominant coalition of voters. Since expenditure and tax decisions impact voter self-interest, information about these decisions (capturable by the accounting system) would be important to voters who would impound the accounting information in their voting decisions. Thus accounting information would be demanded and the design of the accounting system could be determined by examining the voting process in detail.

Furthermore, this research demonstrates that anyone studying the association between accounting numbers and election outcomes must consider the intervening influence of the composition of the voting constituency. Socio-demographic characteristics reflect the composition in terms of population, income, and employment factors. If politicians are concerned about meeting the needs and desires of their constituents, then they will consider such characteristics in formulating fiscal policies. Constituents' desires for public goods and services, reflected in different revenue and expenditure mixes, probably differ among different population, income, and employment groups. Thus research concerned with the association between accounting numbers (which reflect revenue, expenditure, and debt policies) and election outcomes must control for differences in socio-demographic characteristics among cities (as reflective of differing constituent compositions).

## A MORE REALISTIC ENVIRONMENT

The assumptions of perfect, costless information and voter homogeneity are not realistic. As a result, the conclusion that accounting information can be useful in voting decisions is not without debate.

### Costly information

Costly information implies that individual voters cannot afford to collect and assimilate all information that might pertain to their decisions. Since time is a primary resource that must be consumed in information processing, rational economic behavior would dictate that the individual would acquire information as long as its marginal cost, in terms of scarce resources foregone, is less than its marginal return, in terms of the expected gain of voting more "correctly." The magnitude of expected gain could be large if the individual's vote decided the outcome of the election. Since this probability is remote, the magnitude of the expected gain of correct voting is minimal.

Furthermore, as long as the behavior of other voters is independent of the individual voter's decision, the benefits derived by the individual do not depend on his or her choice. In collective choice decisions, no precise relationship exists between individual action and responsibility. In an individual choice situation, the responsibility for and effect of a decision rests with the individual, and thus the individual is motivated to make correct choices. In a collective choice situation, a decision will be made regardless of the individual's actions, and the individual's impact on the results are negligible. Accordingly, the benefits accrue to the individual in spite of his or her decision.

### Costs of incorrect voting

Similarly, the costs of incorrect voting are shared by the constituents. Political decisions may have a negative impact on the constituents' well-being, such as increased taxes or reduced services for segments of the constituency. However, these costs are generally distributed over a large number of individuals, and taken piecemeal, rarely overburden any one segment.[4] Even when political actions are capitalized into property values, the high transaction costs of trading real estate reduce the incentives to closely monitor a politician's actions (see Zimmerman, 1977, for further discussion). On the other hand, the costs (particularly time) of acquiring and processing information are borne directly by the individual voter.[5]

### Uncertain information

Uncertainty about the actions, skills, and performance of politicians leads to incentives for voters to monitor politicians' behavior in order to reduce fraud, embezzlement, or the perquisites consumed by the politician. However, if the monitoring process is costly, voters will find it cost efficient to tolerate a certain amount of divergence between politicians' behavior and their own preferences. As the incentives to monitor politicians' behavior are reduced, the demand for information used in the monitoring process will also be reduced. (For further discussion, see Raman, 1981b, and Zimmerman, 1977.)

In addition, uncertainty impacts the incentive to produce information. Incumbents are motivated to produce information that will assist in their reelection instead of producing information that will reduce voter uncertainty. Zimmerman (1977) suggests that the current governmental accounting format is explainable in light of this motivation. Contemporary fund accounting on the basis of modified accrual permits sufficient reporting flexibility for the politician to produce favorably biased information. Biased reporting enhances the politician's image to constituents, employees, those in other levels of government, and those associated with prospective industry. If municipal financial reports are perceived to be too biased, this information may be discounted by voters as being of little value in assessing past or expected performance. These negative incentives led Downs (1957) to conclude: "Insofar as voting is concerned, any attempt to acquire information beyond that furnished by the stream of 'free' data is for them [citizens] a sheer waste of resources!"


### Information surrogates

Voters employ cost-saving shortcuts in information processing. The use of party affiliation, ideological labels, and demographic descriptors simplify the decision-making process in ways that are consistent with rational decision making. Regardless of the potential value of an information source, voters may find it cost efficient to ignore the source in favor of alternatives. Popkin *et al.* (1976) suggest that voters will be informed when they are able to apply freely available information collected for other purposes (e.g., business activity or investment) to the voting decision or when they are immediately and personally affected by the issues of the election. Certain voters, because of their preoccupation with some issues, will collect and process a substantial amount of information. Most voters, however, will be generally knowledgeable of certain issues and ignorant of many others; for example, voters will often be familiar with information described in newspapers.

## Nonhomogeneous expectations

Voters, even in groups, are not homogeneous. Political parties can be conceived of as coalitions of minorities in which party participation reflects a procedure for obtaining information rather than an expression of loyalty to certain ideals. These hypotheses explain the failure of earlier models of voter behavior (e.g., Campbell *et al.*, 1960) to identify issue-oriented constituencies. Earlier models assumed that voters were well informed, and investigators ascribed the predictive failure of their models to an uneducated or poorly motivated voter. However, being poorly informed may be consistent with rational information processing and is not indicative of a poorly educated or unmotivated public.

Instead of searching out and processing technical information, voters are likely to assess candidates on the basis of more visible signals. The way a candidate looks, talks, and campaigns and his race, age, or religion may be as important as policy issues, which are more nebulous and harder to verify. Also, candidate experience, party affiliation, and style of action have been identified as important factors in voting decisions.

## Asymmetrical information

The production of information for voting decisions is also asymmetrical across candidates. The utility of accounting information for political decisions is severely limited, since it relates only to past performance and thus generally applies only to the incumbent. Regardless of the availability and reliability of accounting information, it can be used only to evaluate the incumbent's performance in office and provides no indication of how an alternative candidate would have performed in the same office. This attribute of governmental accounting information represents a major distinction from information about investment decisions, where much comparative information is available on the choice between securities.

Accounting information collected in a governmental setting provides no standard of comparison. Whereas investors making investment decisions can assess the relative risk-return attributes of alternative assets, voters making election decisions must compare known performance with unknown performance. Investors can compare the performance of securities under similar economic conditions, but voters cannot compare candidates in terms of their performance in the same environment under similar conditions. Voters can compare the financial performance of different entities (e.g., municipalities) in order to assess the relative managerial ability of an incumbent, but there is normally no way of assessing how another politician would have performed under similar circumstances. Thus information asymmetry may influence an election outcome when an incumbent whose past performance is known runs against an opponent whose performance record is not known.

Accordingly, election results are biased in favor of incumbents. For example, Karnig and Walter (1976) report that in 1975, 321 (70 percent) of 456 mayors in jurisdictions with direct elections sought reelection and 210 (65 percent) of the incumbents were reelected. More weight may be placed on competency assessments in voting decisions than on past economic performance. Also, voters may feel that the ability of a candidate to carry out programs, if elected, is as important as the nature of the programs themselves.

Another aspect of the asymmetric nature of political information arises in the context of political campaigns. The magnitude of campaign expenditures differs widely among candidates. All voters will not be equally well informed about all candidates, since different amounts will be spent by the candidates to inform voters of their positions. Campaign expenditures have been shown to significantly affect voting decisions. (For a review of campaign finances and voting behavior, see Adamany, 1977.) Palda (1975) demonstrated that campaign expenditures were significant predictor variables in Canadian provincial elections. For example, in the 1966 Quebec election an incremental dollar of campaign (advertising) expenditure produced a return of one-third vote. Welch (1976) provides a similar study for state elections in Oregon and California.

Thus a number of problems exist for a voter trying to assess the utility he or she can expect to derive from a candidate, for a politician trying to determine the concerns of a constituency, and for anyone trying to assess the relevance of accounting information. Moreover, evaluation of expected utility is not the only decision for a constituent, even for a voter with economic rationality. If a constituent assesses the expected utility from candidate A to be greated than that from candidate B, this does not guarantee that he or she will vote for candidate A. Unless the expected difference is significant to the constituent, he or she may abstain from voting entirely.

### Costs and benefits

In an attempt to predict how an individual would vote and if he or she would vote, Frohlick *et al.* (1978) posited that an important variable is the long-run participation benefit of supporting the democratic process. This study hypothesized a two-candidate, economic voting calculus as follows:

$$(p_1 \times |D|) + (p_2 \times L) - C = U, \tag{3}$$

where $p_1$ is the probability of an individual's vote making a difference in an election outcome, $D$ is the expected differential between candidates, $p_2$ is the probability that the individual's vote will make a difference in the long-run survival of the democratic system, $L$ is the individual's long-run participation value, $C$ is the cost of voting, and $U$ is the net value of voting. The study predicted that a value of $U$ greater than 0 would signal that the individual would vote. A test of the model was made using individual survey data, and a positive association was demonstrated in the 1964 presidential election, indicating that voter participation depends on factors in addition to the evaluation of candidates.

In summary, both theoretical and empirical literature has been cited that questions the objective of accounting as proposed by the AAA Committee (1977), given the real-world conditions under which the accounting system must function. The objective of providing information for voting decisions would appear to be less realistic and may be less productive than more obtainable objectives such as monitoring the stewardship function of management (see Exhibit 3.2).

**Exhibit 3.2**
**Accounting information and election**
**decisions, relaxed assumptions**

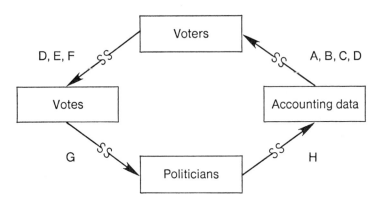

A: Cost-benefit analysis
B: Nonaccounting information
C: Asymmetrical information
D: Uncertainty
E: Party or block affiliation
F: Net benefit exceeds cost of voting
G: Ambiguous signal (coattailing, low turnout)
H: Ambiguous signal (ambiguity of GAAP)

## MUNICIPAL ACCOUNTING INFORMATION AND RESULTS IN ELECTIONS FOR MAYOR

The ability of accounting information to discriminate between election results depends on both the assumptions of economic rationality and the economic conditions that are relevant for a particular constituency. To be discriminating, accounting information must surrogate municipal fiscal policy attributes of interest to voters. Accordingly, accounting numbers may be useful proxies for these policies, which are much harder to identify, measure, and aggregate than are accounting data. Ingram and Copeland (1981c) conducted a direct test of the relationship between accounting variables and election results, as is described below.

## Sample selection and description of clusters

Information about elections for mayor between 1976 and 1978 was obtained by direct correspondence with officials from a national sample of 500 cities with populations exceeding 25,000. The sample was limited to cities with mayor-council forms of government, since mayors under this form generally are elected directly by the voters, while mayors in other forms of government may be appointed or elected by the city council. Hence, mayors in mayor-council governments are not insulated from the voting process. Information was requested about the date of the election, the term of office, and the election result. Two hundred seventy-eight usable responses were received from 364 cities; 86 responses were incomplete, received after the cutoff date, or related to an election for a year in which data were unavailable. Ninety-six additional cities were deleted from the sample because the incumbent ran unopposed or did not run for reelection, leaving two groups that were included in the analysis: (1) 113 cities in which the incumbent was reelected and (2) 69 cities in which the incumbent was defeated.

These cities were clustered into subgroups, each of which was homogeneous in terms of socio-demographic characteristics concerned with population composition, personal income, business activity, and employment concentration.[6] These characteristics previously had been identified in the literature as being capable of distinguishing between constituents' demands for public goods and services. Population composition considered density, race, age, and birthrate. Personal income dimensions were surrogated by median family and per capita income, poverty level, and housing and employment attributes. Economic activity was surrogated by variables concerned with per capita payroll and revenue data from four segments of the economy. Employment concentration concerned the percentage of the population employed in these same segments of the economy. All socio-demographic variables were converted into ratios as a partial control for variations in city size.

Cluster analysis was used to separate the sample of 182 cities into homogeneous groups, with socio-demographic characteristics as clustering variables. The hierarchical clustering procedure identified clusters of cities such that socio-demographic differences between cities within a cluster were minimized. Sixty-two percent of the cities were clustered into three groups, while the remaining cities were clustered into smaller groups of from 1 to 6 cities. The three largest groups consisted of 113 cities, and these were analyzed further.

The mean value for each significant demographic variable provided a basis for characterizing cities within each cluster. Cluster 1 consisted of 31 cities with relatively high population densities, large percentages of nonwhites, low per capita incomes, and low levels of manufacturing, retail, and service business activities. Mayors in 16 of these cities were reelected, while those in 15 were defeated. Cluster 2 included 48 cities with relatively low percentages of nonwhites, high median family and per capita incomes, and high levels of manufacturing and wholesale activity. Twenty-nine of the 48 mayors were reelected, while 19 were defeated. Cluster 3 consisted of 34 cities with low population densities, low median family incomes, high percentages of population below the poverty level, and high levels of retail and service activities. Mayors in 20 cities were reelected, while those in 14 cities were defeated.

### Selection of accounting ratios[7]

Most of the data contained in municipal financial statements fit into one of four categories: revenues, expenditures, debts, and investments. The magnitude of these numbers varies with the size of cities. Ingram and Copeland (1981c) converted all revenue, expenditure, debt, and investment data into financial ratios in order to control for variations in city size. Accounting ratios measured revenue mix (own versus outside revenue, taxes versus user charges), service mix (expenditures), funds flow relationships, and debt requirements. The service mix dimension was represented in two forms, using revenues and expenditures as the denominator. The revenue-based ratios indicated the level of service in relation to the funds required from the constituents, and the expenditure-based ratios indicated the level of service in relation to the total level of services provided by the city.

These categories represented general constructs that captured policy decision differences across cities in revenue sources (the demands placed on constituents for funds), debt burdens (the ability and need to raise funds in the future), liquidity (the ability of the city to provide current services), and the types of services provided.

Thirty-six accounting ratios were calculated for each city for two years, the first fiscal year of the incumbent's term of office and the year preceding the election. Ratios used in the study consisted of the 36 for the year preceding the election and another 36 representing the change in ratios over the incumbent's term of office.

A number of the ratios were similar to those specified in the municipal financial stress literature as being indicative of liquidity or solvency problems (see Clark *et al.,* 1976). Similar ratios were specified as being useful in evaluating credit standing by municipal bond rating agencies (see Sherwood, 1976), and several were employed in bond rating prediction studies (see Michel, 1977). Their potential utility for discriminating between election results was derived from the assumption that accounting numbers reflect the consequences of policy actions regarding public goods and services.

Stepwise discriminant analysis (Eisenbeis and Avery, 1972) was used to identify a parsimonious set of accounting ratios that distinguished between municipalities in which mayors were reelected or not reelected. Independent variables (ratios) entered the model individually and were retained if they contributed to the minimization of Wilk's Lambda. The discriminant procedure "stepped" both forwards and backwards, tested for equality of covariance matrices, and employed linear and quadratic classification functions. Although such empirically derived models were not necessarily optimal ones, they could provide an indication of the ability of the ratios to predict the outcome of elections that would occur in a following year. The classification accuracy and stability of the empirically derived descriptive models were tested using the Lachenbruch procedure. This iterative procedure classified each observation based on a discriminant function computed from the remaining $n - 1$ observations. Data sets for each cluster were subjected to separate stepwise discriminant analyses.

Linear discriminant models were developed, and these identified the 12 financial ratios listed in Exhibit 3.3. For each cluster, the means of ratios that discriminated between election results are presented for each subgroup. The discriminant model for Cluster 1 consisted of 4 significant ratios, while the models for Clusters 2 and 3 included 5 ratios each. The ratios included in the models were predominantly expenditure and debt related. Models for each cluster contained at least 2 expenditure and 2 debt ratios. Ten of the 12 ratios were specified in differenced form, suggesting that the change in revenue or service mixes may be more important discriminators than static measures. Each discriminant model contained at least 1 ratio representing the debt dimension (short-term debt, interest on general debt, total funds to total debt, or general debt). In addition, each discriminant model contained a basic social service ratio (health, welfare, or housing expenditures). In all cases, ratio means for the reelected incumbents indicated that they pursued policies that produced lower levels of debt and higher levels of services than the ratio means for the defeated incumbents.

Cities in Cluster 1 demonstrated high population densities and low income and business activity levels. Those cities with mayors who were not reelected used short-term debt to finance municipal operations and decreased the level of health care and highway services. In contrast, cities with mayors who were reelected reduced reliance on short-term debt financing and reduced health and highway services to a lesser degree than those cities with mayors who were not reelected. Citizens in Cluster 1 cities might be expected to object to a reduction in health care services, since they are likely to be in need of such municipally subsidized services. Reduction of highway expenditures may be seen by citizens as a factor affecting the level of business activity. Increased reliance on short-term financing may be perceived as reflecting fiscal management capabilities or future commitments of tax revenues needed to liquidate a growing debt burden. Reliance on short-term debt has been described as a particularly critical sign of fiscal stress (Sherwood, 1976).

Cluster 2 contained cities with high income levels and high levels of manufacturing and wholesale activities. Cities in Cluster 2 with mayors who were not reelected decreased the commitments for police and health services and had reduced levels of fire services. In contrast, cities with mayors who were reelected increased the municipal commitment to police and health services and had higher

**Exhibit 3.3**

**Means of ratios that discriminate between election results**

*Ratio Means*

| | Cluster 1 | | Cluster 2 | | Cluster 3 | |
|---|---|---|---|---|---|---|
| *Service Functions* | *Reelect* (n=16) | *Defeat* (n=15) | *Reelect* (n=29) | *Defeat* (n=19) | *Reelect* (n=20) | *Defeat* (n=14) |
| Health expenditures/Current expenditures* | −.0008 | −.0029 | .0029 | −.0090 | | |
| Police expenditures/Current expenditures* | | | .0014 | −.0204 | | |
| Housing expenditures/Current expenditures* | | | | | .0095 | .0030 |
| Welfare expenditures/Current expenditures* | | | | | .0002 | −.0006 |
| Welfare expenditures/Total revenue* | | | | | .0001 | −.0004 |
| Highway expenditures/Total revenue* | −.0006 | −.0242 | .0814 | .0603 | | |
| Fire expenditures/Total revenue | | | | | | |
| *Debt Position* | | | | | | |
| Short-term debt/Total revenue* | −.0343 | .0879 | | | | |
| General debt/Total revenue* | −.0326 | .0617 | | | −.0211 | .0923 |
| Short-term debt/Total expenditures* | | | .0094 | −.1275 | | |
| Total funds/Total debt* | | | .0431 | .0219 | −.0036 | −.1624 |
| Interest expenditures/Total revenue | | | | | | |
| Percent correctly classified by discriminant models | 94% | 93% | 90% | 74% | 95% | 86% |

* Change over term of office.
*Source:* Ingram and Copeland (1981c), Tables 4 and 5.

levels of fire services. Citizens of these cities may have perceived these fiscal patterns as reflecting policy commitments to public protection. Demand for these services was positively correlated with income.

Welfare and housing expenditures appeared to be the most important variables in Cluster 3, which consisted of cities with the highest poverty and lowest family income levels. Those cities with mayors who were not reelected increased deficit financing. Welfare expenditures were reduced, and the growth of housing expenditures was lower than for cities whose mayors were reelected. In contrast, cities with mayors who were reelected increased expenditures for welfare and reduced the trend in deficit financing. As was true of the other clusters, the accounting ratios that were most discriminating in Cluster 3 appeared to be consistent with the economic theory of voting and with the attributes of the cities composing the cluster.

The discriminating ability of the ratios was quite high. The Lachenbruch classification results demonstrate that the models were successful discriminators of election results. The model for Cluster 1 produced the best results, with over 93 percent of the 31 observations correctly classified, and the third cluster produced similar results, with an average of 91 percent of 34 observations correctly classified. The second cluster demonstrated poorer results but was still successful in correctly classifying an average of 82 percent of the 48 election outcomes. Results for each cluster were consistent with the notion that accounting ratios discriminate mayoral election results at levels in excess of those expected by change alone.

### Discussion of findings

Findings of the Ingram and Copeland study imply that accounting ratios available one year before an election of a mayor can surrogate voters' perceptions about municipal performance sufficiently to discriminate between election results, given due consideration to socio-demographic characteristics of cities. These results support the contention that municipal accounting ratios provide information of potential use in voting decisions in that the ratios are consistent with voter assessments of the effects of policy decisions.

Different ratios were observed to be significant for different groups of cities. The specific ratios identified by the discriminant analyses are probably less important than the functions they represent—expenditures are primarily a surrogate for the level of services provided to constituencies, and debt is a surrogate for financial stress.

Although few voters are conscious of municipal accounting numbers, most are generally aware of the consequences of an incumbent's fiscal policy decisions, and they impound this information into their voting decisions. The significance of Ingram and Copeland's study is in the demonstrated correspondence of accounting ratios with election outcomes, the visible aspect of voter assessment of municipal financial performance. These results indicate that municipal accounting numbers, in some cases at least, can be considered useful measures of certain aspects of an incumbent's performance.

The study provides evidence that the practical considerations described earlier in this chapter are not sufficient to eliminate the association between accounting measures and voter decision variables. The effect that these considerations have on the linkage is not known. It is probable that noise is introduced into the models as a result of the cost and incentive problems. However, broad generalizability of the study is limited by the restrictions placed on the sample (data availability, election results) and by the procedures used to select the variables and entities for inclusion in the study. Whether or not other ratios or ratios for other samples would demonstrate higher classificatory accuracy is not known. Differences in the accounting systems that produced the accounting numbers were not considered in this study. Modification of the models in order to consider differences in accrual accounting, fixed asset accounting, or pension liability reporting could, with difficulty, be incorporated in future studies.

## SUGGESTIONS FOR FURTHER RESEARCH

Future research might attempt to improve upon the research design used by Ingram and Copeland. More consideration needs to be given to theoretical linkage between accounting ratios and election results. Such a linkage could give direction to the choice of variables and perhaps to the selection of other factors that should be controlled. For example, data about campaign expenditures and political party support might be considered. This data may be available by surveying individual cities or candidates. The study could be extended to other periods and cities in order to expand the sample size and to determine the stability of the results.

Also, future research might extend this study along several different planes. Positive research might attempt to explain mayors' choices of municipal accounting procedures, selection of revenue or expenditure policies, and so on (see Zimmerman, 1977). Descriptive research may consider the association of accounting alternatives with voting outcomes by controlling for specific attributes in selected samples of cities, for example, cash versus accrual basis accounting; mandated independent audits versus no audit; or state-mandated accounting systems versus discretionary systems.

## SUMMARY

This chapter has examined the use of municipal financial information in voting decisions. It has presented evidence that an association exists between accounting information and election choices. However, the results are not sufficient to conclude that present municipal reporting systems are clearly adequate for user needs. In the next chapter, the question of report adequacy is carried into a different decision context, that of investment decisions.

## NOTES

1. As used in this chapter, decision usefulness extends a FASB (1980a) definition from an investment context to a voting decision context: To be useful, ". . . accounting information must be capable of making a difference in a decision by helping users to form predictions about outcomes of past, present, and future events or to confirm or correct expectations" (p. 21). For extended discussions about the traditional

accounting view of decisions and information needs of voters, see Chapter 4 in both volumes of Drebin, Chan, and Ferguson (1981) and Chapter 2 of Anthony (1978).

2. These assumptions are sufficient for economic rationality but are not exhaustive. That is, what motivates voters and politicians may be based on other criteria and may be multifaceted, but the four criteria listed above are assumed to be among the primary motivating elements. These points are summarized from Davis and Haines (1966).

3. For a summary of policy analysis see Dye (1966, 1976) and Sharkansky (1970). Socio-demographic attributes of some cities may act as intervening variables in the election process.

4. Of course, there is the proverbial straw that broke the camel's back. Constituent revolt (Proposition 13-style) to gradual changes in the tax burden is also a real possibility.

5. Zimmerman (1977) has indicated that the role of accounting in a governmental environment is more likely to be as a regulatory device. Since the costs of monitoring a politician's behavior are high and the benefits are low for individual constituents, restrictive procedures are used to constrain political behavior. The accounting system is devised to limit the possible range of actions available rather than to monitor performance. Devices such as budgets and fund accounting limit the possible level of perquisites available to the politician. It is more consistent with current practice to posit the objective of governmental accounting as regulating the behavior of politicians and administrators rather than providing information for voting decisions.

6. Socio-demographic variables for each city were obtained from data reported in the *County and City Data Book* (1978).

7. Accounting data were obtained from data underlying a U.S. Bureau of the Census publication, *City Government Finances*. The Bureau requires a large sample of municipal governments to transcribe their financial statements into a standardized format and report these data to the Bureau each year.

# Chapter Four

# FINANCIAL REPORTING
# FOR MUNICIPAL CREDITORS

One universally recognized objective of municipal financial reporting concerns the disclosure of information that is useful to creditors when they are making investment decisions. Comments of the FASB (1978, par. 37) on the decision needs of creditors are representative:

Financial reporting should provide information to help present and potential . . . creditors . . . in assessing the amounts, timing, and uncertainty of prospective cash receipts from . . . interest and the proceeds from the sale, redemption, or maturity of securities and loans.

The amounts, timing, and uncertainty of cash flows from municipal securities have been subjects of considerable empirical research. Several surrogates for these variables have appeared in the literature, including bond yields, net interest costs, risk premiums, yield variability, yield betas, bond ratings, and changes in bond ratings.

Although the theoretical linkages between accounting information and these surrogates of concern to municipal creditors have not been well specified, much of the empirical research can be described in terms of the following model: Surrogates for amount, timing, uncertaintly of future cash flow $= f$ (security-specific variables, entity-specific variables, other variables). Security-specific variables include such elements of municipal bonds as coupon rate, maturity, sinking fund provision, payment source (general obligation or revenue bonds), call provision, and size of the issue. Entity-specific variables include accounting data and socio-demographic information about the city. Other variables that frequently appear in published research reports include general economic measures or measures of general municipal bond market activity. The functional relationship between variables is most frequently expressed in a linear form. Multiple regression and multiple discriminant analysis are used most frequently to estimate the coefficients for each variable.

The following two sections of this chapter describe some of the institutional attributes of the municipal securities market, since these institutional issues are a dominant part of the research literature. Following sections describe the empirical research linking accounting information with bond ratings, changes in bond ratings, and bond yield surrogates. The concluding section contains an assessment of the extant research and suggestions for future efforts.

## INSTITUTIONAL SETTING

The market for municipal securities is very broad, both in dollar volume and number of issues. Nearly $42 billion of long-term municipal debt was issued through 16,287 separate offerings in 1980 (*Moody's Municipal and Government Manual,* 1981, p. a6). Total state and local debt outstanding at the end of fiscal 1980 was $324 billion, which represented 13 percent of the gross national product (ACIR, 1980, p. 181). Commercial banks owned 41 percent of state and local debt as of 1978, but these institutions generally are prohibited from holding municipal debt that is below investment quality, that is, below a *Baa* rating (see Dougall and Gaumnitz, 1980, p. 166). The broadness of the market reflects several aspects of municipal governments and municipal debt, including but not limited to the following: interest earned by holders of municipal debt is exempt from federal income taxation; approximately 90,000 governmental entities exist, a third of which are empowered to levy taxes; additional symbiotic relationships (beyond the debtor-creditor one) exist between many governments and local investors.

Municipal bond ratings issued by Moody's, Standard & Poor's, and Fitch's rating services represent measures of "debt quality" that are generally reflected in the market as an inverse relationship between rating class and bond yield, that is, the higher the rating, the lower the yield. Although 60 percent of the dollar values of municipal debt are rated by at least one of the services, only 30 percent of the issues are rated at all (Lamb and Rappaport, 1980, p. 72). Bond ratings are not distributed proportionately to the cities throughout the United States. Both the percentage of cities with rated bonds as well as the median bond rating within a state reflect a "state effect." For example, only 41 percent of the cities in Alabama with populations exceeding 10,000 are rated, and the median rating is an *A,* but 100 percent of such cities in Connecticut are rated, and the median rating is an *A*1. The median ratings in Louisiana and Iowa are *Baa* and *Aa* respectively (see Copeland, Ingram, and Magann, 1981, for more detail).

Less than 20 percent of municipal security offerings are brought to market by underwriters who are required to provide information to the public about the offerings in conformity with the Securities Exchange Act of 1934. Even for these securities, disclosures on new municipal bond issues are less extensive than those typically available on new corporate bond issues. Furthermore, secondary trades in municipal bonds occur in the over-the-counter market, in contrast to the trading of corporate bonds on organized exchanges. Thus little information is available on market prices or yields of outstanding municipal bonds. The most comprehensive data on municipal security market activity is available in the *Blue List,* which is published every business day by a division of Standard & Poor's Corporation. The *Blue List* provides data on the security, coupon rate, offering agent, offering yield to maturity, and quantity offered on select issues. Offering yields do not necessarily reflect actual trading yields.

## MUNICIPAL BOND RATINGS

It is commonly believed that municipal investors are concerned with four types of risks: default, marketability, maturity, and business cycle risks (Van Horne, 1978). Default risk measures the probability that principal or interest will not be paid when due. Marketability risk concerns the ability to convert securities into cash before maturity. Maturity risk relates to the expected rate of interest prevailing at the maturity date, and business cycle risk concerns changes in the overall level of yields resulting from general economic fluctuation.

A primary source of information about municipal bond risks is the ratings provided by such rating agencies as Moody's and Standard & Poor's. These agencies evaluate and grade the quality of a bond relative to the probability of default. A rating is initiated upon request of a municipality and requires signing of contracts and payment of fees (ranging from $500 to $3,000). One rating is assigned to all general obligation bonds of a given municipality, although bonds that are not backed by the full faith and credit of the municipality (such as industrial development bonds) are rated individually.

In establishing a rating, a rating agency obtains a comprehensive data set from the municipality that has contracted for a rating (see Sherwood, 1976). The data include 11 components: debt, property valuation, tax valuation, tax revenues, population, annual financial reports, large taxpayers, economic development, school enrollments, borrowing plans, and capital improvement plans. Rating agencies collect data from subscribing municipalities both on a routine basis and prior to each newly proposed offering of securities. However, agencies generally reevaluate rating classifications in conjunction with a new offering. Since most bond rating changes occur in conjunction with a proposed debt offering, ratings may be more relevant for primary rather than secondary bond offerings.

A rating agency usually completes its analysis within five weeks of the receipt of information. Moody's rating announcements (confirmed, revised, or withdrawn) are released in *Moody's Bond Survey* every Monday morning for issues coming to the market during the week. Thus rating announcements are released before publication of the final prospectus. Since one rating is assigned to all general obligation bonds of a given city, a change in rating applies to both the proposed issue and all outstanding general obligation bonds of that city.

All information supplied to rating agencies is not necessarily contained in a prospectus for a new offering, nor has all the information necessarily been widely disseminated. Since the rating or the rating change may reflect "nonpublic" information, a rating change may be an important signal to market participants. Even if the rating change only reflects public information, price adjustments may still be prompted by a rating change if costs to obtain and evaluate information from alternative sources exceed the expected arbitrage gains obtained from the information. Knowledge of a rating or rating change may lower investor information search, acquisition, and evaluation costs if ratings effectively surrogate the information found in a prospectus or other sources. In such cases, rating status could be viewed as an accurate and timely capsulation of new public information. Little empirical evidence is available on this issue. However, Ingram, Brooks, and Copeland (1983) did find that municipal general obligation bonds show a significant yield adjustment in the month of a rating change for both up- and down-rated bonds.

Empirical research indicates that municipal bond ratings were poor indicators of the probability of municipal default prior to the 1940s, and too few municipal bonds have defaulted since then to evaluate the efficacy of ratings as measures of default (see Hempel, 1971).[1] However, Hempel indicates that ratings reflect a less demanding construct of default risk in that yields on securities of cities facing fiscal distress tend to be higher than the median for that rating class. Shannon (1974) provides evidence that municipal ratings capture marketability risk. Maturity risk appears to be preserved within bond rating classes, given that the ordinal relationship of yields is consistent within rating classes for bonds with different term structures (see Robinson, 1960). Van Horne (1978, p. 158) found that the ordinal relationship of yields within rating classes appears to be maintained during changes in the business cycle, for example, the average yields on *Baa* municipal bonds exceeds those of *Aa* bonds during periods of business expansion and recession. Thus municipal bond ratings appear to capture default and marketability risks and preserve the ordinal relationships inherent in maturity and business cycle risks.

## ACCOUNTING INFORMATION AND MUNICIPAL BOND RATINGS

Compared to the number of studies that have been conducted on corporate bond ratings, few empirical studies have examined the relationship between accounting information and municipal bond ratings. Furthermore, the municipal research to date has been substantially less fruitful than the corporate counterpart. The municipal bond rating research can be grouped into two general classes according to the way "accounting information" is surrogated as independent variables. In the first class, the independent variables include accounting ratios. The independent variables in the second class directly measure the presence or intensity of accounting, auditing, or reporting practices. The following paragraphs of this section will briefly describe representative examples of each type of study.

Michel (1977) developed and tested a series of multiple discriminant models in order to predict the general obligation bond ratings for the 45 largest U.S. cities for the period 1967-1971. The independent variables in his final discriminant model included ten financial ratios, each of which was based on data that are typically found in municipal annual reports. Michel estimated model parameters with ratios based on data for the period 1962-1966 and then used these parameters and the ratios for 1967-1971 to predict the ratings for the latter period. His original parameter estimation model correctly classified 60 percent of the 225 observations (45 cities, 1962-1966) and 50 percent of the 225 "holdout" observations (45 cities, 1967-1971). Michel interpreted these results as indicating a low predictive ability, in contrast to the findings of Pinches and Mingo (1973) and others about the relationship between corporate bond ratings and accounting ratios.

Others have conducted similar research on the relationship between accounting ratios and municipal bond ratings (e.g., see Carleton and Lerner, 1969; Morton, 1976; and Raman, 1982), and their findings are generally consistent with those of Michel. However, several key questions about this type of research have been raised, and the success of future efforts will hinge, in part, upon the resolution of these issues. The dependent variable, bond ratings, may in some instances contain misclassifications of the underlying bond risk quality, as is indicated when different ratings are assigned to the same cities by Moody's and Standard & Poor's (see Morton, 1976). Agency ratings measure risk in at least an ordinal manner, regression modeling implies at least an interval measurement, and discriminant modeling implies only a nominal measurement (see Kaplan and Urwitz, 1979). With regard to the independent variables, Pinches (1978) questions the number of variables to be considered and the relationship between the variables. As to the choice of variables, none of the empirical studies of municipal bond ratings has selected as independent variables those data that are known to be collected by the rating agencies, and none has considered including the prior year rating in predicting future ratings, although the probabilities for changes in ratings are asymmetric between rating classes. Of most significance to the development of accounting thought, however, is the issue of whether or not predictions of municipal bond risks (ratings), based upon financial ratios, imply anything about the quality of accounting data. The failure to find strong and reliable relationships between ratios and ratings may reflect a number of potential causes, including the following: faulty research design or execution; the lack of a relationship between historical financial variables considered in the model and future bond risks; and accounting numbers used in constructing ratios that are poor surrogates for the true financial structure of a city. Only this last reason relates directly to the issue concerning the quality of accounting information.

Wallace (1979, 1981a) and Ingram and Copeland (1982a) examined the relationship between bond ratings and accounting variables in a two-stage design. In the first stage, a model was developed that linked bond ratings with financial and socio-demographic variables, and the classification accuracy of the model was noted. In the second stage, additional variables for different aspects of accounting, auditing, or reporting practices were also included in the model, and the incremental impact on classification accuracy was noted. Wallace (1981a) reexamined some of the data from Wallace (1979) and limited her study to an examination of municipal bonds issued from 1974-1976 in the state of Florida. Ingram and Copeland had a larger sample drawn from a more diverse setting, and this study will be described in the remainder of this section.

Ingram and Copeland (1982a) constructed multiple discriminant analysis (MDA) models in order to classify the ratings for 150 municipal bonds and then applied these models in the prediction of ratings for another 150 bonds. The independent variables in one set of models included socio-demographic and financial data about each city, while another set of models contained three additional variables to surrogate state-mandated accounting, auditing, and reporting practices. Using this design, Ingram and Copeland measured the incremental classification accuracy attributable to the state mandates for both the classification and prediction models.

A sample of 300 municipalities was selected for study based on four data-availability criteria. The general obligation bonds of selected cities were rated by Moody's during the period 1975-1978 and experienced no rating change. Financial data on the selected cities were available in a U.S. Bureau of the Census data file underlying the publication, *City Government Finances.* Socio-demographic data were in another census file underlying the publication, *County and City Data Book.* In addition, enough observations per rating class were available so that the analysis might support broad generalizations. Once the sample was selected, it was randomly divided (within rating class) into two subsamples consisting of 150 cities each. The total sample had the following ratings: 134 *Aa,* 131 *A,* and 35 *Baa.* An initial set of 41 socio-demographic and financial variables was obtained for each city. These data were representative of variables that had been used in previous empirical research on municipal bond ratings, rating changes, and interest costs. The large size of the potential independent variable data set reflects an absence of theory on the determinants of municipal security risks, as is discussed by Wallace. Ordinal scales were used to measure the intensiveness of state mandates, as had been previously done by Copeland, Ingram, and Magann (1981). Accounting mandates were represented on a four-point scale:

0 = no state accounting or reporting requirements

1 = state reporting guidelines or standardized report format required

2 = uniform accounting principles and procedures required

3 = both uniform accounting principles and reporting guidelines or standardized report format required

Auditing mandates were represented on a three-point scale:

0 = no state audit required

1 = audit required by state or independent auditor

2 = audit required by independent CPA

Finance mandates were represented on a five-point scale:

0 = no state bond finance requirements

1 = state assists in collecting data on bonded debt

2 = state reviews municipal financial data

3 = state approves data before issuance of securities or pre-scribes data to be reported

4 = state is actively involved in marketing bonds

Information about the mandates for each state were obtained from Petersen, Cole, and Petrillo (1977). Identical mandate scores were assigned to all municipalities in a given state.

Multiple discriminant analysis models were constructed in order to classify the bond ratings for one of the subsamples, using the socio-demographic and financial data as independent variables. The initial MDA model included all 41 financial and socio-demographic variables, but a stepwise iteration procedure sequentially eliminated those that contributed little to the minimization of Wilk's Lambda. Thirteen variables contributed significantly to the model's discriminant ability. Those variables indicated that the lowest-rated municipalities are smaller in area, higher in density, higher in poverty level, higher in per capita debt, lower in revenue per capita, and have a less diversified revenue mix than do higher-rated municipalities. The lowest-rated municipalities have higher ratios of bond and sinking funds to debt and debt service.

The difference in means between the *Aa* and *A* classes are not large for any of the three state mandate variables, but more pronounced differences are found between the means for these classes and those of the *Baa* class.[2] On the average, municipalities with *Aa* or *A* ratings are in states that assist in the collection of data for bond issues and that review these data. Municipalities with *Baa* ratings tend to be located in states that also required state approval prior to financing, prescribed accounting principles or reporting formats, and required independent audits. Thus state involvement in accounting, auditing, and finance practices of municipal governments is greater, on the average, for the lower-rated municipalities.

An MDA model consisting of 13 independent variables representing financial and socio-demographic aspects of cities was constructed, and a 16-variable model was also constructed that included the state mandate surrogates. The classification sample contained the 150 municipalities used to derive model parameters, and the holdout sample contained the remaining 150 municipalities. The holdout sample was used to test the predictive ability of the classification model.

Both models produced similar initial classification results. The 13-variable model correctly classified 78 percent of the sample. The addition of the state mandate variables improved the correct classification rate to 82 percent. Of particular importance is the pattern of misclassifications. Although the classifications of *Aa*- and *A*-rated municipalities frequently were reversed, these municipalities were not misclassified as *Baa*-rated, nor were *Baa* bond misclassified as *Aa* or *A* bonds (i.e., only 1 of the 17 *Baa* municipalities was misclassified in each model). These distinctions are important since bank regulations constrain investments by commercial banks in lower-rated bonds.

The holdout sample results indicated that the model parameters were not stable. The correct classification rate fell to 55 percent for the 13-variable model and to 52 percent for the model containing the state mandate variables. These classification rates were significantly better (at the .05 level) than expected due to chance (41 percent, determined under the proportional chance criterion). Nonetheless, only one of the *Baa* bonds was correctly classified, and the classification accuracy of the models exhibited a dramatic decline (from 78 to 55 percent in the 13-variable model) between classification and holdout samples. The decline in accuracy for the model containing the state mandate variables was even more dramatic (from 82 to 52 percent).

In contrast to these findings, Wallace (1981a) concluded that auditing variables were significantly associated with municipal bond ratings for securities issued in Florida from 1974-1976. However, both the Wallace and the Ingram and Copeland efforts must be considered exploratory studies about the impact of accounting, auditing, and reporting alternatives on attributes that may be of concern to municipal creditors. These studies presume that bond ratings and predictions on bond ratings are of concern to investors. Authorities agree that ratings are of concern to the extent that creditors rely on them as indexes of risk and to the extent that institutional constraints segment the market on the basis of rating classes. Research involving predictions of changes in ratings and direct estimates about future cash flows will be explored in the following sections.

## ACCOUNTING INFORMATION AND MUNICIPAL BOND RATING CHANGES

Several empirical studies have modeled the relationship between accounting ratios and bond rating changes for both municipal and corporate securities. Raman (1981a) considered a sample of 30 cities that experienced a rating change from the *A* class to either the *Aa* or the *Baa* class during the period from 1976-1978. Several discriminant models were constructed and tested on subsamples that were so small that generalization from these findings are extremely tenuous. Copeland and Ingram (1982a) used a larger sample and performed an additional analysis that may have provided more insight into the relationship between accounting measures and bond rating changes. The Copeland and Ingram study will be described as illustrative of this type of research.

Copeland and Ingram employed two empirical analyses to examine the timeliness and reliability of municipal accounting information. Multiple disciminant analysis models were used to assess whether or not municipal accounting measures available prior to a bond rating change could predict the change *and* whether or not municipal accounting measures available subsequent to a change could reflect the economic conditions that initiated the rating change.

A sample of 112 cities that had general obligation bond rating changes (Moody's ratings) during fiscal 1976 was identified. An additional 56 cities that did not experience a bond rating change during the test period (1975-1977) were randomly selected from the population for which data were available. The combined sample of 168 cities was grouped into three classes: 56 cities with no rating change, 35 cities with downgraded ratings, and 77 cities with upgraded ratings.

Revenue, expenditure, debt, and asset data provided the basis for calculating 28 financial ratios considered by Copeland and Ingram.

Financial data were converted into ratios as a partial control for differences in city size. These 28 accounting ratios represented four economic dimensions that might be of concern to municipal creditors: (1) the relative magnitude of debt requirements, (2) the relative magnitude of debt service requirements, (3) the relative magnitude of other expenditures, and (4) the relative magnitude of revenues. Each of the 28 financial ratios was calculated for each of the 168 cities for the years 1975-1977.

In using discriminant analysis, Copeland and Ingram first constructed a series of discriminant models and then tested their accuracy on observations that were not used in the model construction stage. The original specification for the models was in the following form:

$$\text{Group} = f(R_{1t}, R_{2t}, \ldots, R_{28t}),$$

where Group $= 1, 2, 3$ (for the three rating change classes—uprated, unchanged, downrated), $R =$ accounting ratio (1 through 28), and $t$ indicates the time period of the ratio measurement (predate or postdate of the rating event). In null form, the hypothesis tested was: Accounting ratios are no more useful in classifying group membership than chance results.

The two discriminant analyses considered ratios from two different time periods (relative to the date of the rating change). The first analysis used accounting ratios for fiscal years ending prior to the dates of the rating changes. Ratios for fiscal 1975 or 1976 were used with rating changes occurring within 12 months subsequent to the respective fiscal year-end. The second analysis used data for fiscal years ending after the dates of the rating change. Accordingly, ratios for 1976 and 1977 were employed, depending on the fiscal year-end and the date of the change.

The MULDIS discriminant procedure (see Eisenbeis and Avery, 1972) used by Copeland and Ingram "steps" forward and backward and constructs both linear and quadratic discriminant functions. Stepping procedures were employed to reduce the set of 28 ratios to a more parsimonious set of significant explanatory variables. Using MULDIS, independent variables are entered into each model sequentially, in a "step-forward" procedure, and those variables that contribute to a minimization of Wilk's Lambda are retained. Then

MULDIS employs a "step-backward" procedure, which sequentially eliminates individual independent variables that contribute little to the minimization of Wilk's Lambda. Equality of covariance matrices is tested, and linear (quadratic) models are selected as appropriate where equality (inequality) is indicated.

Because of relatively small sample size in the downrated group, the Lachenbruch (Jackknife) classification procedure was used in order to determine the classification accuracy of the discriminant models. This iterative procedure classifies the $i$th observation from a sample of size $n$ (168) based on a classification function derived from the remaining $n - 1$ (167) observations.

Equality of covariance matrices for all discriminant models was rejected and quadratic functions were employed. Eight accounting ratios were contained in the "predictive" quadratic, multiple discriminant function that classified 168 cities in three change groups. In this model, accounting data were available prior to the rating event, and any relationship found indicated "predictive ability" usefulness.

Tests were conducted to assess differences in the eight independent variables across the three groups: an $F$ value of 6.95 indicated significant differences at the .0001 level. The overall classification accuracy of the eight-variable discriminant model was 79 percent at the initial model-formation stage. The uprated and downrated groups were accurately classified, while the unchanged group tended to be substantially misclassified as belonging to the uprated class.

As expected, overall classification accuracy fell in the Lachenbruch stage. However, 55 percent predictive accuracy was achieved, and this is significantly better (.05 level) than the results expected due to chance. The best predictive accuracy was achieved for the uprated and downrated groups, while predictions for the unchanged group were least accurate. The 55 percent predictive accuracy achieved in this test are comparable to results found in studies of predictive accuracy of corporate rating changes, giving due recognition to differences in sample sizes and group structure.

Seven accounting ratios were contained in a quadratic multiple discriminant function that classified 168 cities into three groups, based upon ratios from the period subsequent to the rating event. The relationship found between the accounting variables and the rating groups implies a feedback or confirmation type of usefulness.

An $F$ value of 7.63 was computed (significant at the .0001 level), indicating that the independent variables were significantly different across groups.

The classification accuracy of the seven-variable "feedback" model in the initial model formulation stage, as well as in the Lachenbruch "parameter stability determination" stage, was high. The multiple discriminant function correctly classified 83 percent of the 168 rating changes in the model-building stage, with the accuracy of the downrated and uprated groups exceeding that of the unchanged group. The misclassifications in the unchanged group were most frequently assigned to the uprated group. The overall classification accuracy fell to 70 percent in the Lachenbruch stage, indicating that the model parameters are sensitive to the sample. Classification accuracy substantially improved for the uprated and unchanged groups and marginally declined for the downrated group, as compared to the predictive model results. Seventy percent accuracy is significantly better (at the .05 level) than results expected by chance.

Copeland and Ingram conclude that their results are consistent with the contention that municipal accounting numbers are reliable (*ex post*) measures of the risk attributes reflected by bond rating changes. They contend that municipal accounting information, as currently provided, is much more important in a feedback or confirmation role than in a prediction role. Their results provide only weak support for the contention that accounting data can be used as reliable predictors of bond rating changes. The lack of parameter stability in the predictive models suggests that in making rating decisions rating agencies rely on alternative, more timely, sources of information than are available in published financial statements.

Both the Copeland and Ingram (1982a) and Raman (1981a) studies should be considered exploratory since the discriminant models in both cases did not reflect the asymmetrical costs of misclassification. Decisions based upon misclassifications for the unchanged group involve transaction costs with no potential gain, while potential gain is possible with the other groups. Since the proportion of unchanged cities in the samples for both studies drastically understated the proportion of unchanged cities in the population of all rated cities, the findings from these studies cannot be immediately translated into trading strategies. However, the implications for assessing the quality of municipal accounting disclosures are encouraging. Accounting ratios do seem to capture some of the changes in financial structure of cities that are perceived by rating agencies to have experienced a change in debtor risk attributes.

## ACCOUNTING INFORMATION AND MUNICIPAL BOND YIELD ATTRIBUTES

The magnitude of yields on municipal bonds has changed dramatically during the past few decades, reflecting a growth from approximately 2 percent in the early 1940s to 12 percent in the early 1980s. As briefly described in the first three sections of this chapter, much research has focused on identifying the determinants of municipal bond yields. Accounting surrogates have been used in some of this research as entity-specific independent variables (e.g., see Phelps, 1961; Wallace, 1979, 1981a; and Ingram and Copeland, 1981a, 1982b). Two of these studies will be described in some detail. They are representative of studies in which accounting variables are surrogated by indicator variables and financial ratios.

Wallace (1981a) developed a series of multiple regression models to evaluate the impact of eight accounting and auditing attributes on the net interest cost of 106 municipal bonds issued in Florida from 1974-1976. The basic linear model specified net interest costs as a function of the *Bond Buyer's* bond index, the number of bids submitted, the dealer's spread, an MBIA insurance dummy variable, a bond rating dummy variable, and one of several combinations of eight accounting or auditing dummy variables. The eight accounting or auditing variables indicated whether or not the annual financial reports (1) were audited, (2) were audited by a "Big Eight' firm, (3) were audited by a "private" CPA, (4) received an unqualified audit report, (5) complied with GAAFR, (6) received an MFOA certificate, (7) reflected additional services such as special reports from accountants, and (8) reflected a deficit. Wallace reported results for four iterative regressions that established the relationships between net interest costs and the independent variables: (1) the "basic model" using only financial and demographic independent variables, (2) the basic model plus all eight accounting and auditing variables, (3) the basic model plus the accounting variables, and (4) the basic model plus the auditing variables. The bond rating variable was deleted from the basic model, and the four iterations were replicated in an attempt to assess the impact of any multicolinearity between bond ratings and the accounting-auditing variables. Wallace concluded (p. 511): "While auditing variables do not appear to determine NIC [net interest costs] over and above any impact potentially exerted through its effect on ratings, the accounting variables are relevant in explaining NIC differences across issues."

Wallace's use of dummy variables to surrogate different accounting and auditing practices is potentially fruitful when examining data from relatively small samples. When larger samples are available, a preferable practice would be to divide the total sample into subsamples, each of which would be composed of homogeneous practices that differ between subsamples. Predictive models would be developed on observations for each subsample, and the differences in coefficients for models from different subsamples would provide more insight into the consequences of accounting or auditing alternatives than is available from interpretations of coefficients of dummy variables.

Ingram and Copeland (1981a) evaluated the association between accounting assessment of municipal bond risk and market risk measures. They attempted to predict the systematic bond risk (beta) component of municipal bond yields on the basis of municipal accounting ratios, as has been done frequently in research on corporate securities (see Gonedes and Dopuch, 1974, for a review and critique). Beta is a coefficient that indicates the amount of variation expected in the return (or yield) on a specific security that is associated with the variation in returns for all securities. Security beta may be estimated by regressing over time a security's returns on an index that surrogates market returns.

Beta estimates have been made on portfolios of municipal securities by Schneeweis (1977) and Hoffland (1972). However, market returns for specific securities must be available in order to estimate betas for individual securities, and little data are available for municipal securities that are traded in the over-the-counter market. Ingram and Copeland (1981a) attempted to overcome this problem with a five-step procedure. First, data on the yield to maturity, coupon rate, and maturity date of bonds were obtained from the *Blue List* for general obligation bonds of 127 cities, as of the last day of each month for 31 months (from August 1976 to February 1979). Separate sets of regression parameters for maturity and coupon rates were estimated for each month by subjecting observations for all issues for an individual month to a cross-sectional regression. Using these parameters, an adjusted yield was developed for each security by subtracting the maturity and coupon effects from the original yields to maturity. A mean return per month per city was obtained by averaging multiple returns for those cities that had more than one security listed in a given month. Finally, the systematic time-series component of returns, beta, was estimated for each city by regressing each return against an index (the equally weighted average of returns for all 127 cities). The 127 betas represent *ex post* estimates of systematic risk.

Ten accounting ratios were calculated for each city for the years 1974, 1975, and 1976. These ratios were designed to capture the relative magnitude of municipal debt, debt service requirements, other expenditure requirements, and the adequacy of revenues. The ten accounting ratios, with the addition of bond ratings, were used to make one-, two-, and three-year-ahead predictions of systematic risk for the 127 cities; that is, ratios for fiscal years 1974-1976 were used to predict the estimated betas. Linear multiple regression models were used to make the predictions. The adjusted $R^2$ for the one-year-ahead estimates was .445. The level of association deteriorated for the two- and three-year-ahead predictions, as expected. Nevertheless, the $R^2$s for all three time periods were significant at the .01 level and were higher than comparable results obtained in previous studies that linked accounting ratios with corporate betas. The authors concluded that their evidence was consistent with the contention that municipal accounting information can be useful to municipal creditors in estimating future levels of market risk.

The studies by Wallace (1979, 1981a) and Ingram and Copeland (1981a) provide direct evidence about the quality of municipal accounting information, when quality is interpreted as implying decision usefulness. Both studies found persistent and significant relationships between accounting variables and security return variables, notwithstanding the pervasive qualitative deficiencies of municipal accounting information documented in Chapter 2 of this book. If municipal accounting information is of questionable quality (e.g., does not conform to GAAP), why is it associated with decision variables (e.g., market risk measures)? Ingram and Copeland attribute this finding to the fact that relatively few sources of financial information on municipal performance are available. Thus investors may be forced to rely on accounting data even if it is not of high quality.

## IMPACT OF SELECTED ACCOUNTING METHODS ON BOND ATTRIBUTES

Does the selection of accounting methods used by a municipality have an impact on its bond rating or yield attributes? The Wallace (1979, 1981a) and the Ingram and Copeland (1981a) studies described above represent only a few of the many research efforts currently seeking an answer to this question. Similar research has examined state-mandated accounting variables and municipal bond yield attributes (Ingram and Copeland, 1982b), lease capitalization practices and municipal bond ratings (Perry, 1982b) municipal pension recognition practices and both bond risk and yields (Copeland and Ingram, 1982b), and "preferred" accounting practices for state governments and state bond yields (Ingram, 1983). Most of these studies employ a general model as follows:

Bond attribute $= f$(Accounting variables, Other variables),

and the samples consist of entities that use a variety of accounting alternatives. This body of research is one of such recent origin that it has not received the critical exposure of peer review needed to refine methodological procedures. But critical review is inevitable, so that more and better research on the crucial question is bound to appear in the future.

## SUMMARY

The quality of municipal financial disclosures may be considered from the perspective of municipal creditors. If municipal creditors are concerned with information that is useful for assessing the amounts, timing, and risks associated with future cash flows, they may be interested in predictions of bond ratings, changes in bond ratings, yields, and measures of systematic risk. This chapter has described several studies that attempted to relate municipal accounting variables with these market attributes. The accounting variables used in these studies were surrogated in terms of financial ratios and dummy variables. Multiple linear regression or discriminant analysis were often used to estimate the model coefficients from one sample, and these models predicted outcomes for holdout samples. In general, the empirical relationships found in the literature between accounting variables and municipal bond ratings were weaker than those found in corporate bond studies but are still statistically significant. Although stronger and more reliable relationships were found between accounting surrogates and changes in bond ratings, the evidence from one study suggests that accounting information serves the more important function of confirming the existence of the underlying changes in financial structure that trigger the changes in ratings. Furthermore, accounting and auditing variables have been linked with attributes of market yields, such as net interest costs and systematic risk. A growing body of research is being directed toward measuring the impact of selected accounting methods on bond attributes.

The results of this body of research are tentative. However, the preliminary results are encouraging in that accounting information appears to be of some use in making credit decisions.

Further research must be conducted in order to confirm the results found in these initial efforts. Three separate lines of research should prove fruitful: model development, descriptive-predictive studies of bond attributes, and measurement of the impact of selected accounting methods on bond attributes. Model development research might consider the impacts of alternative measurement specifications (e.g., ordinal vs. cardinal measures for bond rating surrogates, standardized vs. unstandardized ratios); alternative selection of variables; alternative relationships between variables (e.g., linear vs. nonlinear models); alternative data sets (e.g., annual report data, Moody's data, or census data), and alternative controls for exogenous influences. Since many of the studies cited in this chapter were conducted with data from extremely small samples, direct replication on expanded samples would be a significant contribution.

## NOTES

1. Hempel (1971, p. 112) states: "Only six rated state and local issues defaulted since the 1929 major default period. All six were limited liability obligations." A few general obligation municipal defaults did occur in the mid 1970s, e.g., New York and Cleveland.
2. For example, the mean index of state accounting mandates for the *Aa*-rated bonds was 1.94 (on a 0 to 3 scale), while the index for the *Baa* bonds was 2.47.

*Chapter Five*

# SUMMARY, DISCUSSION,
# AND CONCLUSIONS

The primary objective of this book has been to review a broad cross section of literature bearing on the issue of municipal financial disclosure quality so that interested readers can obtain a comprehensive overview of a complex subject. The previous chapters have described a variety of studies found in the accounting, finance, economics, public administration, and political science literatures. Although the focus of each study differs, the implications of their findings suggest directions for future accounting policy decisions and accounting research. In this chapter we briefly summarize the literature on four topics that are closely related to those described in the previous chapters. Next, we recapitulate our analysis and reiterate the implications drawn from the survey.

## LITERATURE ON FOUR RELATED TOPICS

Four topics that we have not explicitly considered are closely related to those described in the previous chapters: municipal efficiency and effectiveness, population migration, the determinants of municipal revenues and expenditures, and municipal fiscal stress. Much has been published on each of these topics, and selected bibliographies are included in this book for those who are interested in a broader consideration of issues bearing on the quality of municipal accounting disclosures. Although page constraints prevent us from providing detailed descriptions of research on these topics, the following sections do present a brief overview.

## Municipal efficiency and effectiveness

Most municipal managers and many employees use accounting information in the performance of their functions, at least to the extent that they prepare or use budgets and receive or disburse funds. Few municipal managers routinely employ budgeting and accounting data to measure organizational efficiency and effectiveness (as is commonly done in business), but current interest in these issues is ascending. Potentially, municipal accounting can play a role in specifying objectives, establishing goals for budgets, establishing standards, appraising performance, and evaluating alternatives. That is, the planning, control, and decision-making functions of municipal operations can be enhanced through the design of accounting systems and complete exploitation of the potential disclosure capabilities of accounting reports.

The municipal accounting literature is much more advanced than the general state of municipal accounting practice. The literature concerned with municipal efficiency and effectiveness is very broad, and no single taxonomy can produce exhaustive and exclusive classifications. Under one scheme, the literature can be classified in terms of conceptual discussions,[1] case studies,[2] surveys of accounting techniques or research findings,[3] practical "how to do it" guides,[4] and bibliographies.[5] Another taxonomy might consider selected accounting techniques designed to enhance efficiency or effectiveness, such as programmed budgeting,[6] zero-based budgeting,[7] productivity bargaining,[8] internal control,[9] performance auditing,[10] or capital budgeting.[11] Other classifications can also be devised.

In general, the literature indicates that specific techniques do have the potential for enhancing municipal efficiency and effectiveness, and some have been implemented successfully at one time or another in many cities. However, our reading of the literature leads us to conclude that most of the available innovations are implemented infrequently, the expected benefits are rarely realized, and the innovations are soon abandoned. Perhaps the combined recession and taxpayer revolt of the early 1980s will stimulate more governments to consider some of the methods described in the literature.

## Population migration

Tiebout (1956) posited that individuals move freely among political jurisdictions in order to maximize satisfaction (as was described more fully in Chapter 3). It is assumed that these individuals have full knowledge of revenue and expenditure patterns in cities that are considered as potential homesites. Each city offers a different package of public goods and services to its residents. Presumably, potential residents can learn about the package of public goods and services that is being offered by a city directly from the city's budgets and annual financial statements or indirectly from secondary reports about these documents (e.g., newspaper articles). In turn, each city will assume fiscal characteristics that reflect its economic base, and these attributes may also be reflected in the annual budgets and financial statements. In such an environment, the quality of municipal financial disclosure can play a role in attracting or repelling potential residents.

Tiebout's theory has been subjected to much empirical research. Although the empirical results of many studies generally support Tiebout's hypothesis, limitations in design for most of the studies prevent us from gaining insight into the relationship between population mobility and the quality of municipal disclosure. However, the designs and findings of a few studies might be of interest to accounting researchers. Aronson and Schwartz (1973) developed a model of population migration based on differences in financial performance across municipalities. Forecasts were derived to predict the relative change in municipal populations. Population changes in towns adjacent to Harrisburg, Pennsylvania, were tested, and a significant proportion of the population shifts were predicted correctly. Local expenditure and tax data were used as independent variables in the predictive model. Reschovsky (1979) also found that local revenue and expenditure factors influenced residential choice decisions. Differential effects were noted across different economic classes, thus indicating a correspondence between the socioeconomic composition of citizens and the city's economic base. A similar model might be used in accounting research to exploit different demands for information expected from different socioeconomic groups.

Another aspect of the population migration research concerns the relationship between housing prices and the quality of public goods and services provided by cities. In a study of direct relevance to accounting research, Epple and Schipper (1981) examined the relationship between the price of housing and municipal pension funding practices. Since unfunded municipal pension liabilities typically are not disclosed with other municipal liabilities on the face of the financial statements, a test of funding practices also implies a test of disclosure practices. Studying the design of this research definitely can provide insight for those persons interested in exploring further the relationship between the quality of municipal accounting disclosure and population migration.

## The determinants of municipal revenues and expenditures

An extremely large body of literature has examined the relationship between socio-demographic variables and revenues and/or expenditures for various types of governmental entities. Many of the early studies that followed Fabricant's (1952) seminal research applied a similar methodology: multiple regression analysis developed cross-sectional models that attempted to explain the variation in many surrogates for governmental expenditures. Three types of criticisms were leveled at the early determinants literature: the studies lacked theoretical structure; the studies generally considered revenues or expenditures for a single level of government when often state, local, and federal agencies had concurrent programs that focused on one function; and the independent variable set contained two or more variables that were jointly determined by other variables. Critics claimed that the lack of theory led to specification error in which important variables were completely ignored. The aggregation problem was addressed by considering overlapping activities of different governmental entities. Some researchers did address the simultaneity problem by developing and solving simultaneous equations for related variables (for example, see Horowitz, 1968).

Both the methodological and substantive issues raised in this body of research should be of interest to accounting researchers. Many of the accounting studies cited in the previous chapters use similar variables in similar models. Accountants can improve their research by adopting some of the procedures that are now commonly applied in the public finance literature. The "determinants" literature does describe theories, models, and variables that can be used in research on the quality of municipal disclosures.

## Municipal fiscal stress

Accounting reports generally are presumed to describe with reasonable accuracy the financial condition and results of operations of specific entities. Thus the quality of municipal accounting was seriously questioned by the national reports of widespread, unexpected, and disastrous fiscal conditions faced by many cities during the 1970s. The label *municipal fiscal stress* was applied to a variety of real and imagined conditions by a variety of commentators. Some critics claimed that municipal financial reports failed to indicate the deteriorating financial condition of cities approaching bankruptcy, to the permanent detriment of several constituent groups. The actual credit defaults of New York City and Cleveland tended to legitimatize some of this criticism.

Much has been written about municipal fiscal stress. For example, the selected bibliography in Burchell and Listokin (1981) contains references to approximately 400 books, reports, and articles devoted to fiscal stress, and these tend to be limited to the very recent studies or to "classic" references. Thousands of pages have been written about the fiscal crises of New York City alone. Despite this plethora of published materials on fiscal stress (or possibly because of it), several crucial issues have not been resolved: What is municipal fiscal stress? How is it to be measured? What underlying causes create stress? and How can stress be prevented or reversed? Our brief review of the literature will consider each of these issues in turn.

Several different concepts of fiscal stress have been discussed in the literature, and these can be described as lying along a continuum with varying degrees of broadness.[12] A narrow definition of stress might be limited to a formal declaration of bankruptcy, while the broadest definition might be concerned with an unfulfilled demand for public goods and services. Much of the literature on New York City did concentrate on the narrow definition, but most of the fiscal stress literature considered broader issues, since no city has been formally declared bankrupt since the end of the Great Depression. Examples of concepts that fall between the extremes include the following: credit default; insolvency or an excess of liabilities over assets; an excess of cash outflows over cash inflows; a significant deterioration in the time series of selected financial indicators, for example, revenue or debt trends; a city-suburb relative measure of fiscal disparity; and an unfulfilled demand for vital public goods and services. Obviously, the appropriateness of a fiscal stress measure hinges upon which concept is under consideration, but many different measures have been developed for each concept. Accounting data have been used in many studies of fiscal stress as either dependent or independent variables. Obviously, the extent of fiscal stress found in each study is a function of definition and measurement, in addition to bias introduced in the sampling plan. The search for underlying causes and solutions to municipal fiscal stress generally suffers from a deficiency of theory, although the "efficiency," "migration," and "determinants" literatures all identify theories that are applicable. Most authors agree that stress is a complex condition. This complexity poses a major problem to those engaged in empirical research on fiscal stress: simple models ignore vital variables, relationships, and joint effects, while estimation error (resulting from surrogating variables from "soft" data) confounds the interpretation of findings from complex models. Nevertheless, several practical guides have been devised to measure the extent of stress, and "tried and true principles of sound management" have been suggested as potential remedies.[13]

## SUMMARY

Several public and private organizations influence the specification of municipal financial reporting standards. The decentralized approach to establishing standards, coupled with the absence of an effective enforcement mechanism, promote an environment conducive to reporting diversity. Substandard reporting quality is one potential consequence of permissive diversity. Reporting diversity also hampers the ability of users to make cross-sectional comparisons, and it opens to question policy actions predicated on such comparisons. Many published complaints about the "low quality" of municipal financial disclosures are found in the literature, but most of these have been based upon observations from limited samples. One factor complicating the interpretation of these negative evaluations is that disclosure quality can be measured against different standards. Quality judgments can concern the extent of disclosure, compliance of disclosures with established standards, and the usefulness of disclosures to selected groups of municipal constituents. According to the consensus of opinion, the ultimate determinant of disclosure quality, and hence the index of prime concern, focuses on how useful information is to decision makers.

Chapter 2 summarized research that evaluated municipal reporting practices relative to the explicit standards provided by generally accepted accounting principles. All of the studies cited in the chapter document the pervasive noncompliance with generally accepted accounting principles for governmental entities. Several survey studies described opinions of various user groups concerning their perceptions about the usefulness of municipal disclosures in satisfying their decision needs. Most of this research supported the contention that users are not fully satisfied with contemporary municipal disclosures. Some of this survey research indicated that many users question the potential effectiveness of alternative policy actions for improving disclosure quality. They also reflected an awareness of the relative contribution of institutional factors that induce disclosure practices that are of questionable quaity. Chapter 2 also described a few studies that indicated the difficulty of using currently available municipal financial data in making inter-city comparisons. Most of the research cited in this chapter supported the contention that current disclosure practices are deficient and could be improved to better meet users' needs.

In Chapter 3 we described a large body of literature that examines the usefulness of municipal disclosures for voting decisions. The "positive theory" of voter and incumbent behavior suggests a number of conceptual issues that might reduce the usefulness of accounting data for making election choices. However, the empirical research on predicting election results with models based on municipal accounting information demonstrated relatively high degrees of predictive accuracy with consistent reliability. Since few studies have focused on the voter decision-making process from an accounting perspective, much more research must be undertaken before definitive conclusions are reached. Yet the preliminary evidence suggests that accounting information does reflect critical aspects of municipal policy choices that influence voters' decisions.

Chapter 4 extended the examination of decision usefulness to an investment context. Research was summarized that assessed the association between municipal accounting data and bond ratings, bond rating changes, bond yields, and market measures of bond risk. This research demonstrated that the association between reported accounting data and bond ratings is reliable (i.e., statistically significant) but not especially strong (i.e., only of moderate predictive accuracy). The association between accounting ratios and rating changes is higher but still not sufficient to support profitable security trading strategies. In fact, it appears as though the reported accounting information may lag rating changes. Accounting information appears to be associated with market measures of bond risk and with bond yields. These results suggest that investors may consider the financial information in their investment decisions. Rating agencies appear to rely upon other informaiton (in addition to accounting data) in determining ratings.

## DISCUSSION

Several caveats must be considered in evaluating the research summarized in the previous chapters. Each of the studies reviewed has some methodological ambiguities and limitations that restrict generalization of the findings. Some of these problems are indicated in this book, while others are documented in the underlying literature. Accordingly, any conclusions drawn from specific findings must be considered tentative. However, recurrent and consistent findings were observed in several studies, and these may be accepted with somewhat greater confidence. A high degree of agreement exists on most of the points presented in our summary above.

Many of the studies described in this book were designed to examine specific issues within specific contexts, and some did not attempt to consider accounting policy issues. In fact, many were not written from an accounting perspective. Thus it is difficult and sometimes tenuous to draw accounting policy implications from these studies. Inferences may not be generalizable beyond a specific context.

Furthermore, the ability to draw accounting policy implications from these studies suffers from a lack of explicit cost-benefit criteria for measuring information value. Even if the results clearly indicate that current municipal accounting information is useful for external user decisions, a mechanism does not exist for assessing the benefits of using the information relative to the costs of deriving, reporting, and assessing the information. In addition, no mechanism exists for comparing the net costs of the present institutional environment with some alternative.

As final caveat, the reader should recognize the relatively recent emergence of accounting interest in empirical municipal research. Although approximately 40 percent of the bibliography references to empirical research on municipal issues cited in this book are found in accounting publications, most of these have been published since the mid 1970s.[14] (In contrast, much empirical municipal research was published in the economics and public finance literature during the past 30 years.) If accounting research continues at its current pace, new studies on each of the issues we have described will be available in the near future.[15] In all likelihood, some of the findings will contradict those reported here. Thus the reader should expect to find a continued stream of published empirical evidence bearing on the quality of municipal disclosure. Final judgment on disclosure quality is premature at this point in time.

Given these caveats, what implications can be drawn from the research surveyed? First, it seems apparent that the current reporting environment encourages diverse reporting practices. In the short run, the inter-city comparability aspect of disclosure quality can be improved by altering practices to conform to standards or modifying standards to conform to practices. The pervasiveness of diverse practice suggests that a modification of the environment is needed in order to facilitate a long-run conformity between standards and practice. Since state governments do have the right to mandate municipal accounting practices, federal intervention may be required to achieve uniformity of reporting practices.[16] An environmental change less drastic than federal intervention may be sufficient to achieve a greater degree of conformity than presently exists.[17] In any event, neither the costs nor benefits of obtaining greater conformity between accounting standards and reporting practices has been approximated.

Given the failure of many cities to comply with existing reporting standards, it is difficult to determine whether or not the information produced according to those standards would have met the needs of specific users. Before serious consideration is given to changing reporting standards, much more thought must be devoted to developing enforcement mechanisms. Otherwise, a change in standards will not necessarily improve disclosure quality. Institutional efforts other than quasi-regulatory fiat might prove effective. For example, rating penalties for poor disclosure by bond rating agencies will raise interest rates and lower the availability of credit for those cities that fail to comply with GAAP.[18] Little is known at this time about the existing relationship between quality of disclosure and interest costs or credit availability.

Much of the empirical research described in the preceding chapters employed accounting ratios and numbers as independent variables in modeling or predicting selected outcomes. From an accounting perspective, interpretative ambiguity exists in evaluating findings about the linkages between dependent and independent variables. Should the accounting ratios be considered as surrogates for some underlying economic phenomena, or are they surrogates for the outputs of accounting systems? If the former, then little is learned about accounting per se. Much more accounting research that explicitly differentiates accounting and economic phenomena is needed. Future municipal accounting research might be structured along the lines of the corporate accounting research that is designed to measure the impact of a change in accounting method or principle, so that direct evidence on accounting issues will be obtained.

An interesting subject for additional research concerns the differences in information content of reported data for municipalities that comply with current standards vis-à-vis those that do not comply. For example, if the association between investment decisions and accounting data is stronger for complying entities than for non-complying entities, current standards may have a meaningful effect on disclosure quality.

Another implication of the research surveyed in this book is that at least some accounting information produced in the current institutional environment is useful in some decision contexts. The association between reported data and bond risk measures appears to be significant. Similarly, an association exists between the data and election outcomes. Thus municipal financial disclosures appear to be relevant for external users' needs. The current institutional environment does not eliminate this relevance. On the other hand, the strength of identified associations has not been sufficiently strong to rule out improvements in disclosure quality. In particular, the timing of municipal disclosures appears to hinder its relevance. Accounting data was found to be more useful, *ex post,* as a feedback mechanism for bond rating changes than, *ex ante,* as a predictive device. Since municipalities often do not report financial information until well after the end of the fiscal period, policymakers might consider alternatives to facilitate more timely reporting.

A final implication of this research review is that considerable research should be directed toward determining the decision needs and data requirements of external users. Relatively little theory exists that specifies how or why various types of information is used. Most empirical research relies on ad hoc models or *a priori* theory. The rigorous financial and economic theories that are frequently applied to corporate accounting data often are not relevant in a nonprofit environment. Most of the research that has been done in the municipal sector has searched for empirical relationships without the advantage of a strong conceptual foundation.

## CONCLUSIONS

A considerable body of research exists that examines issues relevant to municipal accounting policy choices. Most of the research is found outside of the accounting literature and is not intended as an evaluation of accounting information or policy decisions. Nevertheless, the research employs accounting data in assessing the effect of municipal performance and management behavior on external users' decisions.

Relatively little of this research has been noted in the accounting literature. Furthermore, only recently have the research paradigms and methodologies common in corporate accounting research been applied in the municipal sector. The need and potential for research involving municipal accounting issues are apparent.

Results to date have been encouraging. Many of the methodologies applied in other sectors also provide significant findings when applied to municipal data. Research findings generally are interpretable in light of the idiosyncrasies of the municipal disclosure environment. We are optimistic that future efforts will sufficiently extend the base of empirical knowledge so that it becomes a factor of value in policy decisions.

## NOTES

1. See Charnes and Cooper (1980); Sorensen and Grove (1977).
2. See National Center for Productivity (1977).
3. See Gambino and Reardon (1981); Brace *et al.* (1980); Greiner *et al.* (1981).
4. See Washnis (1980); Hatry *et al.* (1977).
5. See *Guide to Productivity Improvement Projects* (1976); Katzell *et al.* (1977).
6. See Schick (1966).
7. See *Zero-Based Budgeting* (1977).
8. See Horton (1976).
9. See Wallace (1981b).
10. See Comptroller General of the United States (1981); Henke (1973).
11. See Steiss (1975).
12. The introduction to Burchell and Listokin (1981, pp. xi-li) traces the theoretical and empirical themes concerned with municipal fiscal stress from the early 1950s to the present. Brief descriptions and references to each of the ideas presented in our overview are to be found on these pages. Burchell and Listokin provide further amplification on pages 159 to 230.

13. For example, see Rosenberg and Stallings (1978); Kordalewski (1978).
14. Although the bibliography is not exhaustive, it is representative.
15. In fact, several have already appeared since the first draft of this book was written, as indicated in the last section of Chapter 2.
16. Federal intervention might take the form of direct regulation of disclosures or indirect regulation related to issuing municipal securities, obtaining federal funds, etc.
17. The ultimate effectiveness of the proposed GASB will not be known for some time.
18. As is currently being done by Standard & Poor's Corporation (1980).

# SELECTED BIBLIOGRAPHY

## STUDIES OF MANAGERIAL EFFICIENCY AND EFFECTIVENESS

Brace, P.; R. Elkin; D. Robinson; and H. Steinberg. *Reporting of Service Efforts and Accomplishments.* Stamford, Conn.: Financial Accounting Standards Board, 1980.

Caldwell, K. "Efficiency and Effectiveness Measurement in State and Local Government." *Governmental Finance,* November 1973, pp. 19-21.

Charnes, A., and W. Cooper. "Auditing and Accounting for Program Efficiency and Management Effectiveness in Not-for-Profit Entities." *Accounting, Organizations and Society* 5 (1980): 87-108.

Comptroller General of the United States. *Standards for Audit of Governmental Organizations, Programs, Activities and Functions.* Washington, D.C.: General Accounting Office, March 1981.

"Employee Performance Standards and Appraisals." *State and County Administrator,* July/August 1976, pp. 16-20.

Feild, H. "Traits in Performance Ratings—Their Importance in Public Employment." *Public Personnel Management,* September/October 1975, pp. 327-330.

Fountain, J., and R. Lockridge. "Implementation and Management of a Performance Auditing System." *Governmental Finance* 5 (1974): 12-21.

Gambino, A., and T. Reardon. *Financial Planning and Evaluation for the Nonprofit Organization.* New York: National Association of Accountants, 1981.

Greiner, J.; H. Hatry; M. Koss; A. Millar; and J. Woodward. *Productivity and Motivation: A Review of State and Local Government Initiatives.* Washington, D.C.: Urban Institute, 1981.

*Guide to Productivity Improvement Projects.* 3rd ed. Washington, D.C.: International City Management Association, 1976.

Hasby, C., and H. Steinberg. *Performance Auditing — Toward Meaningful Financial Management.* Special Bulletin 1975D. Chicago: Municipal Finance Officers Association, 1975.

Hatry, H., *et al. How Effective Are Your Community Services?: Procedures for Monitoring the Effectiveness of Municipal Services.* Washington, D.C.: Urban Institute, 1977.

Hawley, W., and D. Rogers, eds. *Improving the Quality of Urban Management.* Beverly Hills, Calif.: Sage, 1974.

Hayes, F. *Productivity in Local Government.* Lexington, Mass.: D.C. Heath, 1977.

Henke, E. "Performance Evaluation for Not-for-Profit Organizations." *Journal of Accountancy,* June 1973, pp. 51-55.

Horton, R. "Productivity and Productivity Bargaining in Government: A Critical Analysis." *Public Administration Review,* July-August 1976, pp. 407-414.

*Improving Government Productivity: Selected Case Studies.* Washington, D.C.: National Center for Productivity and Quality of Working Life, 1977.

*Improving Management of the Public Work Force: The Challenge to State and Local Government.* New York: Committee for Economic Development, 1978.

Katz, H. "The Municipal Budgetary Response to Changing Labor Costs: The Case of San Francisco." *Industrial and Labor Relations Review,* July 1979, pp. 506-519.

Katzell, R., P. Bienstock, and P. Faerstein. *A Guide to Worker Productivity Experiments in the United States: 1971-1975.* New York: New York University Press, 1977.

Matson, M. "Capital-Budgeting — Fiscal and Physical Planning." *Governmental Finance,* August 1976, pp. 42-48.

McBride, H. "Benefit-Cost Analysis and Local Government Decision-Making." *Governmental Finance,* February 1975, pp. 31-34.

Mercer, J. "Five-Year Operating Budget." *Governmental Finance,* February 1973, pp. 30-31.

Moore, P. "Types of Budgeting and Budgeting Problems in American Cities." *International Journal of Public Administration,* 1980, pp. 501-514.

*Productivity of People: Grant Projects in Human Resource Management.* Washington, D.C.: U.S. Civil Service Commission, BIPP 152-85, September 1977.

Schick, A. "The Road to PPB: The Stages of Budget Reform." *Public Administration Review,* December 1966, pp. 243-258.

Sorenson, J., and H. Grove. "Cost-Outcome and Cost-Effectiveness Analysis: Emerging Nonprofit Performance Techniques." *The Accounting Review,* July 1977, pp. 658-675.

Steiss, A. *Local Government Finances: Capital Facilities Planning and Debt Administration.* Lexington, Mass.: D.C. Heath, 1975.

Usher, C., and G. Cornia, "Goal Setting and Performance Assessment in Municipal Budgeting." *Public Administration Review,* March/April 1981, pp. 229-235.

Wallace, W. "Internal Control Reporting Practices in the Municipal Sector." *The Accounting Review,* July 1981b, pp. 666-689.

Washnis, G., ed. *Productivity Improvement Handbook for State and Local Government.* New York: Wiley, 1980.

*Zero-Based Budgeting.* Washington, D.C.: U.S. Office of Management and Budget, Bulletin No. 77-9, April 19, 1977.

## STUDIES OF POPULATION MOBILITY

Aronson, J., and E. Schwartz. "Financing Public Goods and the Distribution of Population in a System of Local Governments." *National Tax Journal,* June 1973, pp. 137-159.

Bahl, R., and D. Greytak. "The Response of City Government Revenues to Changes in Employment Structure." *Land Economics,* November 1976, pp. 415-434.

Bradford, D., and H. Kelejian. "An Econometric Model of the Flight to the Suburbs." *Journal of Political Economy,* May-June 1973, pp. 566-589.

Buchanan, J., and C. Goetz. "Efficiency Limits on Fiscal Mobility: An Assessment of the Tiebout Model." *Journal of Public Economics,* April 1972, pp. 25-43.

Cebula, R. "Interstate Migration and the Tiebout Hypothesis: An Analysis According to Race, Sex, and Age." *Journal of the American Statistical Association,* December 1974, pp. 876-879.

Clotfelter, C. "Spatial Rearrangement and the Tiebout Hypothesis: The Case of School Desegregation." *Southern Economic Journal,* October 1975, pp. 263-270.

Edel, M., and E. Sclar. "Taxes, Spending and Property Values: Supply Adjustment in the Tiebout-Oates Model." *Journal of Political Economy,* September-October 1974, pp. 941-954.

Ellsott, R. "Fiscal Impacts on Intermetropolitan Residential Location: Further Insights on the Tiebout Hypothesis." *Public Finance Quarterly,* April 1980, pp. 189-212.

Fredland, D. "A Model of Residential Change." *Journal of Regional Science,* August 1975, pp. 199-208.

Gillespie, W. "Effect of Public Expenditures on the Distribution of Income." In R. Musgrave (ed.), *Essays on Fiscal Federalism.* Washington, D.C.: Brookings Institution, 1965.

Granfield, M. "Residential Location: A Comparative Econometric Analysis." *Applied Economics,* June 1974, pp. 95-108.

Greene, J., W. Neenan, and C. Scott. *Fiscal Interactions in a Metropolitan Area.* Lexington, Mass.: D.C. Heath, 1974.

Hamilton, B. "Property Taxes and the Tiebout Hypothesis: Some Empirical Evidence." In E. Mills and W. Oates (eds.), *Fiscal Zoning and Land Use Controls: The Economic Issues.* Lexington, Mass.: D.C. Heath, 1975.

————. "Capitalization of Intrajurisdictional Differences in Local Tax Prices." *American Economic Review,* December 1976, pp. 743-754.

Harris, R., G. Tolley, and C. Harrell. "The Residential Site Choice." *Review of Economics and Statistics,* May 1968, pp. 241-247.

Haskell, M., and S. Leshinski. "Fiscal Influences on Residential Choice: A Study of the New York Region." *Quarterly Review of Economics and Business,* Winter 1969, pp. 47-55.

Oates, W. "The Effects of Property Taxes and Local Public Spending on Property Values: An Empirical Study of Tax Capitalization and the Tiebout Hypothesis." *Journal of Political Economy,* November-December 1969, pp. 957-971.

Pollakowski, H. "The Effects of Property Taxes and Local Spending on Property Values: A Comment and Further Results." *Journal of Political Economy,* July-August 1973, pp. 996-1003.

Reschovsky, A. "Residential Choice and the Local Public Sector: An Alternative Test of the 'Tiebout Hypothesis,' " *Journal of Urban Economics,* 1979, pp. 501-519.

Sacks, S., and J. Callahan. "Central City-Surburban Fiscal Disparity." *City Financial Emergencies: The Intergovernmental Dimension.* Washington, D.C.: U.S. Advisory Commission on Intergovernmental Relations, 1973.

## DETERMINANTS OF REVENUES AND EXPENDITURES

Bahl, R. "Fabricant's Determinants after Twenty Years: A Critical Reappraisal." *American Economist,* Spring 1966, pp. 27-44.
————. "Intraurban Interactions, Social Structure, and Urban Government Expenditures: A Stochastic Model." *Social Economic Planning Sciences,* December 1969, pp. 179-290.
Bahl, R., and R. Saunders. "Determinants of Changes in State and Local Government Expenditures." *National Tax Journal,* March 1965, pp. 50-57.
————. "Factors Associated with Variations in State and Local Government Spending." *Journal of Finance,* September 1966, pp. 523-534.
Booms, B. "City Governmental Form and Public Expenditure Levels." *National Tax Journal,* June 1966, pp. 187-199.
Brazer, H. *City Expenditures in the United States.* Washington, D.C.: National Bureau of Economic Research, 1959.
Davies, B., A. Barton, and I. McMillan. "Variations in the Provisions of Local Authority Welfare Services for the Elderly; A Comparison between County and Borough." *Social and Economic Administration,* April 1971, pp. 100-124.
Fabricant, S. *The Trend of Governmental Activity in the United States since 1900.* New York: National Bureau of Economic Research, 1952.
Fisher, G. "Interstate Variations in State and Local Government Expenditures." *National Tax Journal,* March 1964, pp. 55-74.
Gabler, L., and J. Brest. "Interstate Variations in Per Capita Highway Expenditures." *National Tax Journal,* March 1967, pp. 78-85.
Hansen, N. "The Structure and Determinants of Local Public Investment Expenditures." *Review of Economics and Statistics,* May 1965, pp. 150-162.
Hawley, A. "Metropolitan Population and Municipal Government Expenditures in Central Cities." *Journal of Social Issues* 7 (1951): 100-108.
Horowitz, A. "A Simultaneous Equation Approach to the Problem of Explaining Interstate Differences in State and Local Expenditures." *Southern Economic Journal,* April 1968, pp. 459-476.
Kurnow, E. "Determinants of State and Local Expenditures Reexamined." *National Tax Journal* 16 (1963): 252-255.
Liebert, R. "Municipal Functions, Structure and Expenditures: A Reanalysis of Recent Research." *Social Science Quarterly,* March 1974, pp. 765-783.
Morss, E. "Some Thoughts on the Determinants of State and Local Expenditures." *National Tax Journal,* March 1966, pp. 95-103.

Morss, E., J. Friedland, and J. Hymans. "Fluctuations in State Expenditures: An Econometric Analysis." *Southern Economic Journal,* April 1967, pp. 496-517.

Osman, J. "Determinants of Interstate Variations in Capital and Current Outlays by State and Local Governments." *The Annals of Regional Science,* June 1969, pp. 125-134.

Sacks, S., and R. Harris. "The Determinants of State and Local Government Expenditures and Intergovernmental Flow of Funds." *National Tax Journal,* March 1964, pp. 75-85.

Spangler, R. "The Effect of Population Growth upon State and Local Government Expenditure." *National Tax Journal,* June 1963, pp. 193-196.

Stephens, G., and H. Schmandt. "Revenue Patterns of Local Governments." *National Tax Journal,* December 1962.

Sunley, E. "Some Determinants of Government Expenditures within Government Areas." *American Journal of Economics and Sociology* 30 (1971): 345-364.

Tiebout, C. "A Pure Theory of Local Expenditures." *Journal of Political Economy,* August 1956, pp. 416-424.

## STUDIES OF FISCAL STRESS

Alcaly, R., and D. Mermelstein, eds. *The Fiscal Crisis of American Cities: Essays on the Political Economy of Urban America with Special Reference to New York.* New York: Random House, Vintage Books, 1977.

Allman, T. "The Urban Crisis Leaves Town." *Harper's,* December 1978, pp. 41-56.

Aronson, J. "Is There a Fiscal Crisis Outside of New York?" *National Tax Journal,* June 1978, pp. 153-163.

Bish, R. *The Public Economy of Metropolitan Areas.* Chicago: Markham, 1971.

Black, J. *The Changing Economic Role of Central Cities.* Washington, D.C.: Urban Institute, 1978.

Blair, J., and D. Nachmias, eds. *Fiscal Retrenchment and Urban Policy.* Beverly Hills, Calif.: Sage, 1979.

Burchell, R., and D. Listokin, eds. *Cities under Stress.* Newark, N.J.: Center for Urban Policy Research, Rutgers, 1981.

*City Financial Emergencies.* Washington, D.C.: Advisory Commission on Intergovernmental Relations, 1973.

Clark, T., I. Rubin, L. Pettler, and E. Zimmerman. *How Many New Yorks? The New York Fiscal Crisis in Comparative Perspective.* Research Report No. 72. Chicago: Comparative Study of Community Decision Making, University of Chicago, 1976.

Colman, W. *Cities, Suburbs, and States: Governing and Financing Urban America.* New York: Free Press, 1975.

Conroy, M. *The Challenge of Urban Economic Development: Goals, Possibilities, and Policies for Improving the Economic Structure of Cities.* Lexington, Mass.: Lexington Books, 1975.

Galambos, E., and A. Schreiber. *Making Sense Out of Dollars: Economic Analysis for Local Government.* Washington D.C.: National League of Cities, 1978.

Gorham, W., and N. Glazer, eds. *The Urban Predicament.* Washington, D.C.: Urban Institute, 1976.

Groves, S., M. Godsey, and M. Shulman. "Financial Indicators for Local Government." *Public Budgeting and Finance,* Summer 1981, pp. 5-19.

Hovey, H. *Development Financing for Distressed Areas.* Washington, D.C.: Northeast-Midwest Institute, 1979.

Howell, J., and C. Stamm. *Urban Fiscal Stress: A Comparative Analysis of 66 U.S. Cities.* Lexington, Mass.: Lexington Books, 1979.

Hubbell, L., ed. *Fiscal Crisis in American Cities: The Federal Response.* Cambridge, Mass.: Ballinger, 1979.

Kordalewski, J. *Ways of Identifying Cities in Distress.* Washington, D.C.: Urban Institute, 1978.

Meyer, J., and J. Quigley. *Local Public Finance and the Fiscal Squeeze: A Case Study.* Cambridge, Mass.: Ballinger, 1977.

Muller, T. *Growing and Declining Urban Areas: A Fiscal Comparison.* Washington, D.C.: Urban Institute, 1975.

*Municipal Fiscal Indicators: An Information Bulletin of the Management, Finance and Personnel Task Force of the Urban Consortium.* Washington, D.C.: U.S. Department of Housing and Urban Development, 1980.

Nathan, R., and C. Adams. "Understanding Central City Hardship." *Political Science Quarterly* 91 (1976): 47-62.

National League of Cities. *State of the Cities: 1975, A New Urban Crisis?* Washington, D.C.: 1976.

Petersen, J. "Simplification and Standardization of State and Local Government Fiscal Indicators." *National Tax Journal,* September 1977, pp. 299-311.

Peterson, G., *et al. Urban Fiscal Monitoring.* Washington, D.C.: Urban Institute, 1978.

Pettengill, R., and J. Uppal. *Can Cities Survive? The Fiscal Plight of American Cities.* New York: St. Martin's Press, 1974.

Puryear, D., *et al.* "Fiscal Distress: An Imbalance between Resources and Needs." *Occasional Papers in Housing and Community Affairs.* Washington, D.C.: U.S. Department of Housing and Urban Development, July 1979, pp. 148-168.

Rosenberg, P., and W. Stallings. *Is Your City Heading for Financial Difficulty: A Guidebook for Small Cities and Other Governmental Units.* Chicago: Municipal Finance Officers Association, 1978.

Schlosstein, R. "Older 'Core Cities' Economies Pose Fiscal Problems for State and Local Governments." *Tax Review,* July 1976, pp. 25-28.

"Urban Fiscal Problems." *National Tax Journal,* September 1976, entire issue.

## OTHER MAJOR REFERENCES

Ackoff, R. "Towards a Behavioral Theory of Communication." *Management Science* 4 (1958): 218-234.

Adamany, D. "Money, Politics and Democracy: A Review Essay." *American Political Science Review,* 1977, pp. 289-304.

Advisory Commission on Intergovernmental Relations. *Federal Grants: Their Effects on State-Local Expenditures, Employment Levels, Wage Rates.* Washington, D.C.: ACIR, February 1977, A-61.

―――. *Significant Features of Fiscal Federalism.* Washington, D.C.: ACIR, 1980.

American Accounting Association. "Report of the Committee on Accounting in the Public Sector, 1974-1976." Supplement to *The Accounting Review* 52 (1977): 33-52.

American Institute of Certified Public Accountants. *Audits of State and Local Governmental Units.* New York: AICPA, 1974.

―――. *Accounting Trends & Techniques.* New York: AICPA, annual.

Anthony, R. *Financial Accounting in Nonbusiness Organizations.* Stamford, Conn.: Financial Accounting Standards Board, 1978.

Arcelus, F., and A. Meltzer. "The Effect of Aggregate Economic Variables on Congressional Elections." *American Political Science Review,* December 1975, pp. 1232-1239.

Asher, H. *Causal Modeling.* Beverly Hills, Calif.: Sage, 1976.

Bachrack, S., and H. Scoble. "Mail Questionnaire Efficiency: Controlled Reduction of Nonresponse." *Public Opinion Quarterly,* Summer 1967, pp. 265-271.

Baron, C. "The Distribution and Timeliness of the Annual Municipal Financial Report." Working Paper No. 12, Public Sector Section, American Accounting Association, July 1978.

Barr, A., J. Goodnight, J. Sall, and J. Hellwig. *A User's Guide to SAS.* Raleigh: North Carolina State University Press, 1979.

Beaver, W., J. Kennelly, and W. Voss. "Predictive Ability as a Criterion for the Evaluation of Accounting Data." *The Accounting Review,* October 1968, pp. 675-683.

Bloom, H., and H. Price. "Voter Response to Short-Run Economic Conditions: The Asymmetric Effect of Prosperity and Recession." *American Political Science Review,* December 1975, pp. 1240-1254.

Boyette, A., and G. Giroux. "The Relevance of Municipal Financial Reporting to Municipal Security Decisions." *Governmental Finance,* May 1978, pp. 29-35.

Buzby, S. "Selected Items of Information and Their Disclosure in Annual Reports." *The Accounting Review,* July 1974, pp. 423-435.

Campbell, A., P. Converse, W. Miller, and D. Stokes. *The American Voter.* New York: Wiley, 1960.

Carleton, W., and E. Lerner. "Statistical Credit Scoring of Municipal Bonds." *Journal of Money, Credit and Banking,* November 1969, pp. 750-764.

Cerf, A. *Corporate Reporting and Investment Decisions.* Berkeley and Los Angeles: University of California Press, 1961.

Cockrill, R.; M. Meyerson; J. Savage; E. Keller; and M. Maher. *Financial Disclosure Practices of the American Cities.* New York: Coopers & Lybrand, 1976.

Copeland, R., and R. Ingram. "Municipal Financial Reporting Deficiencies: Causes and Solutions." *Governmental Finance,* November 1979, pp. 21-24.

———. "The Association between Accounting Information and Municipal Bond Rating Changes." *Journal of Accounting Research,* Autumn 1982a.

———. "Market Recognition of Unfunded Municipal Pension Fund Liabilities." Working Paper 82-9, Northeastern University, April 1982b.

Copeland, R.; R. Ingram; and J. Magann. "Some Preliminary Evidence on a Positive Theory of Municipal Disclosure." *Proceedings of the Southeast American Accounting Association Meeting,* April 1981.

Davis, O., and G. Haines. "A Political Approach to a Theory of Political Expenditures: The Case of Municipalities." *National Tax Journal,* September 1966, pp. 259-275.

Davis, O., and M. Hinich. "A Mathematical Model of Policy Formation in a

Democratic Society." In J. Bernd (ed.), *Mathematical Applications in Political Science II*. Dallas: Southern Methodist University Press, 1966.

Dhaliwal, D. "Improving the Quality of Corporate Financial Disclosure." *Accounting and Business Research*, Autumn 1980, pp. 385-391.

Dougall, H., and J. Gaumnitz. *Capital Markets and Institutions*. Englewood Cliffs, N.J.: Prentice-Hall, 1980.

Downs, A. "An Economic Theory of Political Action in a Democracy." *Journal of Political Economy*, April 1957, pp. 135-150.

Drebin, A., J. Chan, and L. C. Ferguson. *Objectives of Accounting and Financial Reporting for Governmental Units: A Research Study*, Vol. 1 and 2. Chicago: National Council on Governmental Accounting, 1981.

Dye, T. *Politics, Economics, and the Public: Policy Outcomes in the American States*. Chicago: Rand McNally, 1966.

———. *Policy Analysis*. University: University of Alabama Press, 1976.

Eisenbeis, R., and R. Avery. *Discriminant Analysis and Classification Procedures*. Lexington, Mass.: D. C. Heath, 1972.

Engstrom, J. "Perceived Information Needs of Municipal Budget Participants." Working Paper No. 9, Public Sector Section, American Accounting Association, May 1978.

Epple, D., and K. Schipper. "Municipal Pension Funding: A Theory and Some Evidence." *Public Choice*, 37 (1981): 141-178.

Ernst & Whinney. *How Cities Can Improve Their Financial Reporting*. Cleveland: Ernst & Whinney, 1979.

Evans, J., and J. Patton. "An Economic Analysis of Participation in the Municipal Finance Officers Association Certificate of Conformance Program." Pittsburgh, University of Pittsburgh Working Paper, November 1981.

Financial Accounting Standards Board. *Objectives of Financial Reporting by Business Enterprises*. Stamford, Conn.: FASB, 1978.

———. *Qualitative Characteristics of Accounting Information*. Stamford, Conn.: FASB, 1980a.

———. *Elements of Financial Statements of Business Enterprises*. Stamford, Conn.: FASB, 1980b.

Fiorina, M. "Economic Retrospective Voting in American National Elections: A Micro-Analysis." *American Journal of Political Science*, 1978, pp. 426-443.

Firth, M. "The Impact of Size, Stock Market Listing, and Auditors on Voluntary Disclosure in Corporate Annual Reports." *Accounting and Business Research*, Autumn 1979, pp. 273-280.

Frohlich, N.; J. Oppenheimer; J. Smith; and O. Young. "A Test of Downsian

Voter Rationality: 1964 Presidential Voting." *American Political Science Review,* 1978, pp. 178-197.

Gjesdal, F. "Accounting for Stewardship." *Journal of Accounting Research,* Spring 1981, pp. 208-231.

Gonedes, N., and N. Dopuch. "Capital Market Equilibrium, Information Production, and Selecting Accounting Techniques: Theoretical Framework and Review of Empirical Work." Supplement to *Journal of Accounting Research* 12 (1974): 48-129.

Governmental Accounting Standards Board Organization Committee. *Report of the Governmental Accounting Standards Board Organization Committee.* Exposure Draft, February 16, 1981.

Graber, D. "Personal Qualities in Presidential Images: The Contribution of the Press." *Midwest Journal of Political Science,* 1972.

Greenball, M. "The Predictive Ability Criterion: Its Relevance in Evaluation of Accounting Data." *Abacus,* June 1971, pp. 1-7.

Grove, H., and R. Savich. "Attitude Research in Accounting: A Model for Reliability and Validity Considerations." *The Accounting Review,* July 1979, pp. 522-537.

Hall, J., and P. Piele. "Selected Determinants of Precinct Voting Decisions in School Budget Elections." *Western Political Quarterly,* 1974, pp. 440-456.

Hansen, E. "Municipal Finances in Perspective: A Look at Inter-Jurisdictional Spending and Revenue Patterns." Supplement to *Journal of Accounting Research* 15 (1977): 156-162.

Haseman, W., and R. Strauss. "The Quality of Financial Reporting by General Purpose Local Governments." In A. Drebin, J. Chan, and L. Ferguson (eds.), *Objectives of Financial Reporting for Governmental Units: A Research Study,* Vol. 2. Chicago: NCGA, 1981.

Hastie, K. "Determinants of Municipal Bond Yield." *Journal of Financial and Quantitative Analysis,* June 1972, pp. 1729-1748.

Hempel, G. *The Postwar Quality of State and Local Debt.* New York: National Bureau of Economic Research, 1971.

Hoffland, D. "The Price-Rating Structure of the Municipal Bond Market." *Financial Analysts Journal,* March-April 1972, pp. 65-70.

Holder, W. *A Study of Selected Concepts for Governmental Financial Accounting and Reporting.* Chicago: Municipal Finance Officers Association, 1980.

Howard, T., and D. Johnson. "Municipal Financial Reports for the 1980s." *Public Budgeting & Finance,* Winter 1981, pp. 80-84.

Ijiri, Y., and R. Jaedicke. "Reliability and Objectivity of Accounting Measurements." *The Accounting Review,* July 1966, pp. 474-483.

Ingram, R. "The Importance of State Accounting Practices for Creditor Decisions." *Journal of Accounting and Public Policy* 2 (1983): forthcoming.

Ingram, R., L. Brooks, and R. Copeland. "The Information Content of Municipal Bond Rating Changes." *Journal of Finance,* 1983, forthcoming.

Ingram, R., and R. Copeland. "Modeling Auditor Assessments of Municipal Disclosure Problems." Collected Papers, *American Accounting Association Annual Meeting.* 1979, pp. 69-82.

———. "The Association between Accounting Numbers and Market Risk of Municipal Bonds." Columbia: University of South Carolina Working Paper, 1981a.

———. "Disclosure Practices in Audited Financial Statements of Municipalities." *Public Budgeting & Finance,* Summer 1981b, pp. 47-58.

———. "Municipal Accounting Information and Voting Behavior." *The Accounting Review,* October 1981c, pp. 830-842.

———. "State Mandated Accounting, Auditing, and Finance Practices and Municipal Bond Ratings." *Public Budgeting & Finance,* Spring 1982a, pp. 19-29.

———. "Municipal Market Measures and Reporting Practices: An Extension." *Journal of Accounting Research,* Autumn, 1982b, forthcoming.

———. "Bibliography on Accounting and Municipal Pension Fund Liabilities." Working Paper 82-8, Northeastern University, April 1982c.

Kaplan, R., and G. Urwitz. "Statical Models of Bond Ratings: A Methodological Inquiry." *Journal of Business,* April 1979, pp. 231-261.

Karnig, A., and B. Walter. "Municipal Elections: Registration, Incumbent Success, and Voter Participation." *Urban Data Service Reports,* Vol. 8. Washington, D.C.: International City Management Association, 1976.

Kerlinger, F. *Foundations of Behavioral Research.* 2nd ed. New York: Holt, Rinehart and Winston, 1973.

Kramer, G. "Short-Term Fluctuations in U.S. Voting Behavior, 1896-1964." *American Political Science Review,* March 1971, pp. 131-143.

Lamb, R., and S. Rappaport. *Municipal Bonds.* New York: McGraw-Hill, 1980.

Libby, R., and B. Lewis. "Human Information Processing Research in Accounting: The State of the Art." *Accounting, Organizations and Society* 2 (1977): 245-268.

Louderback, J. "Projectability as a Criterion for Income Determination Methods." *The Accounting Review,* April 1971, pp. 298-305.

Luthy, D. "Municipal Financial Reporting: The Importance of Selected Items of Information and a Measure of Consensus." Working Paper No.

13, Public Sector Section, American Accounting Association, August 1978.

Maher, M., and E. Keller. "An Analysis of Reporting Practices in American Cities." Paper presented at the National Meeting of the American Accounting Association, Denver, 1978.

Marshak, J. "Economic Theory of Information." Working Paper No. 118, Western Management Science Institute, UCLA, May 1967.

Maschmeyer, R., and R. Van Daniker. "Information Needs of State and Local Officials." *Governmental Finance,* November 1979, pp. 15-19.

May, G. *Financial Accounting.* New York: Macmillan, 1943.

McDonald, D. "Feasibility Criteria for Accounting Measures." *The Accounting Review,* October 1967, pp. 662-679.

Meltzer, A., and M. Vellrath. "The Effects of Economic Policies on Votes for the Presidency: Some Evidence from Recent Elections." *Journal of Law and Economics,* December 1975, pp. 781-798.

Michel, A. "Municipal Bond Ratings: A Discriminant Analysis Approach." *Journal of Financial and Quantitative Analysis,* November 1977, pp. 587-598.

Mock, T. "Concepts of Information Value and Accounting." *The Accounting Review,* October 1971, pp. 765-778.

————. *Measurement and Accounting Information Criteria.* Sarasota, Fla.: American Accounting Association, 1976.

*Moody's Municipal and Governmental Manual,* Vol. 1. New York: Moody's Investor Service, 1981.

Morton, T. "A Comparative Analysis of Moody's and Standard & Poor's Municipal Bond Ratings." *Review of Business and Economic Research,* Winter 1976, pp. 1-18.

Municipal Finance Officers Association. *Disclosure Guidelines for State and Local Government.* Chicago: MFOA, 1980.

————. "Response to the Report of the Governmental Accounting Standards Board Organization Committee." Chicago: MFOA, 1981a.

————, Committee on Accounting and Financial Reporting. "A Response to the NCGA Holder Study." *Governmental Finance,* March 1981b, pp. 26-31.

*Municipal Year Book.* Washington, D.C.: International City Management Association, annual.

National Committee on Governmental Accounting. *Governmental Accounting, Auditing and Financial Reporting.* Chicago: NCGA, 1968.

National Council on Governmental Accounting. *Statement 1: Governmental Accounting and Financial Reporting Principles.* Chicago: NCGA, 1979.

————. *Statement 3: Defining the Governmental Reporting Entity.* Chicago: NCGA, 1982.

Oppenheim, A. *Questionnaire Design and Attitude Measurement.* New York: Basic Books, 1966.

Palda, K. "The Effect of Expenditures on Political Success." *Journal of Law and Economics,* 1975, pp. 745-771.

Parry, R. "The Effects of Lease Capitalization on Municipal Debt Disclosures." *Public Budgeting & Finance,* Spring 1982a, pp. 30-39.

————. "The Impact of Leasing Information on a Statistical Scoring Model for Municipal Bond Ratings." Paper presented at the National Meeting, American Accounting Association, San Diego, Calif., August 1982b.

Parry, R., and S. Webster, "City Leases: Up Front, Out Back, In the Closet." *Financial Analysts Journal,* September-October 1980.

Petersen, J., L. Cole, and M. Petrillo. *Watching and Counting: A Survey of State Assistance to and Supervision of Local Debt and Financial Administration.* Chicago: MFOA, 1977.

Petersen, J., *et al. State and Local Government Finances and Financial Management: A Compendium of Current Research.* Washington D.C.: MFOA, 1978.

Phelps, C. "The Impact of Tightening Credit on Municipal Capital Expenditures in the United States." *Yale Economic Essays,* Fall 1961, pp. 275-321.

Pinches, G. "Classification Results and Multiple Discriminant Analysis." Lawrence: University of Kansas Working Paper, September 1978.

Pinches, G., and K. Mingo. "A Multivariate Analysis of Industrial Bond Ratings." *Journal of Finance,* March 1973, pp. 1-18.

Popkin, S.; J. Gorman; C. Phillips; and J. Smith. "Comment: What Have You Done for Me Lately? Toward an Investment Theory of Voting." *American Political Science Review,* 1976, pp. 779-805.

Raman, K. "The Tiebout Hypothesis: Implications for Municipal Financial Reporting." *Journal of Accounting, Auditing & Finance,* Fall 1979, pp. 31-41.

————. "Financial Reporting and Municipal Bond Rating Changes." *The Accounting Review,* October 1981a, pp. 910-926.

————. "Municipal Financial Reporting: 'Managing' the Numbers." *Public Budgeting & Finance,* Autumn 1981b, pp. 56-61.

————. "Relative Usefulness of a Municipal Operating Statement: A Survey." *Proceedings of the Southwest American Accounting Association,* March 1981c, pp. 183-191.

————. "Financial Reporting and Municipal Bond Ratings." *Journal of Accounting, Auditing & Finance,* Winter 1982, pp. 144-153.

Robinson, R. *Postwar Market for State and Local Government Securities.* Princeton, N.J.: National Bureau of Economic Research, 1960.

Rosenfield, P. "Stewardship." In J. Cramer and G. Sorter, (eds.), *Objectives of Financial Statements: Selected Papers.* New York: AICPA, 1974.

Sacks, S., and R. Harris. "The Determinants of State and Local Government Expenditures and Intergovernmental Flow of Funds." *National Tax Journal,* March 1964, pp. 75-85.

Schneeweis, T. "Bond Ratings as a Measure of Market Risk." *Proceedings of the National Tax Association—Tax Institute of America Joint Conference,* 1977, pp. 334-339.

Shannon, D. "Some Evidence of Imperfections in the Market for Municipal Bonds." *The Financial Review,* 2 (1974): 64-78.

Shapiro, M. "Rational Political Man: A Synthesis of Economic and Social-Psychological Perspectives." *American Political Science Review,* 1969, pp. 1106-1119.

Sharkansky, I. *Policy Analysis in Political Science.* Chicago: Markham, 1970.

Sherwood, H. *How Corporate and Municipal Debt Is Rated.* New York: Wiley, 1976.

Simon, H.; H. Guetzkow; G. Kozmetsky; and G. Tyndall, *Centralization and Decentralization in Organizing the Controller's Department.* New York: Controllership Foundation, 1954.

Singhvi, S., and H. Desai. "An Empirical Analysis of the Quality of Corporate Financial Disclosure." *The Accounting Review,* January 1971, pp. 129-138.

*Standard & Poor's Policy Statement: Municipal Accounting and Financial Reporting.* New York: Standard & Poor's Corporation, November 26, 1980.

*Standard & Poor's Policy Statement: Municipal and International Bond Ratings.* New York: Standard & Poor's Corporation, 1978.

Stigler, G. "General Economic Conditions and National Elections." *American Economic Review,* May 1973, pp. 160-167.

Tiebout, C. "A Pure Theory of Local Expenditures." *Journal of Political Economy,* October 1956, pp. 416-424.

Tufte, E. "Determinants of the Outcomes of Midterm Congressional Elections." *American Political Science Review,* September 1975, pp. 812-826.

U.S. Bureau of the Census. *City Government Finances.* Washington, D.C.: Government Printing Office, 1972-1978.

———. *County and City Data Book.* Washington, D.C.: Government Printing Office, 1972-1978.

Van Daniker, R., and K. Pohlmann. *Exposure Draft of a Research Report: Preferred Accounting Practices for State Governments.* Chicago: NCGA, 1982

Van Horne, J. *Financial Market Rates and Flows*. Englewood Cliffs, N.J.: Prentice-Hall, 1978.

Wallace, W. "The Effect of State Accounting and Auditing Regulations on Municipal Borrowing Costs and Bond Ratings." Paper presented at the Round Table Conference on Government Regulation of Accounting and Information, University of Florida, 1979.

————. "The Association between Municipal Market Measures and Selected Financial Reporting Practices." *Journal of Accounting Research,* Autumn 1981a, pp. 502-520.

Welch, W. "The Effectiveness of Expenditures in State Legislative Races." *American Politics Quarterly,* 1976, pp. 333-356.

Zimmerman, J. "The Municipal Accounting Maze: An Analysis of Political Incentives." *Studies on Measurement and Evaluation of the Economic Efficiency of Public and Private Nonprofit Institutions.* Supplement to the *Journal of Accounting Research* 15 (1977): 107-144.

# AUTHOR INDEX

Ackoff, R., 12, 120
Adamany, D., 66, 120
Advisory Commission on Intergovernmental Relations, 80, 119, 120
Alcaly, R., and D. Mermelstein, 118
Allman, T., 118
American Accounting Association, 55, 67, 120
American Institute of Certified Public Accountants, 4, 5, 9, 31, 120
Anthony, R., 19, 77, 120
Arcelus, F., and A. Meltzer, 60, 120
Aronson, J., 118
Aronson, J., and E. Schwartz, 101, 115
Asher, H., 54, 120

Bachrack, S., and H. Scoble, 39, 121
Bahl, R., 117
Bahl, R., and D. Greytak, 115
Bahl, R., and R. Saunders, 61, 117
Baron, C., 48-50, 121
Barr, A., J. Goodnight, J. Sall, and J. Hellwig, 121
Beaver, W., J. Kennelly, and W. Voss, 20, 121
Bish, R., 118

Black, R., 118
Blair, J., and D. Nachmias, 118
Bloom, H., and H. Price, 60, 121
Blue List, 81, 95
Booms, B., 117
Boyette, A., and G. Giroux, 40-42, 54, 121
Brace, P., R. Elkin, D. Robinson, and H. Steinberg, 110, 113
Bradford, D., and H. Kelejian, 115
Brazer, H., 117
Buchanan, J., and C. Goetz, 115
Burchell, R., and D. Listokin, 103, 110, 118
Buzby, S., 48, 121

Caldwell, K., 113
Campbell, A., P. Converse, W. Miller, and D. Stokes, 60, 65, 121
Carleton, W., and E. Lerner, 84, 121
Cebula, R., 61, 115
Cerf, A., 48, 121
Charnes, A., and W. Cooper, 110, 113
Clark, T., I. Rubin, L. Pettler, and E. Zimmerman, 71, 119
Clotfelter, C., 116

# SUBJECT INDEX